T0329295

ECONOMIC PROBLEMS
OF DEMOCRACY

ECONOMIC PROBLEMS
OF DEMOCRACY

BY

ARTHUR TWINING HADLEY

PRESIDENT-EMERITUS OF YALE UNIVERSITY,
MEMBER OF THE AMERICAN ACADEMY OF ARTS AND LETTERS
CORRESPONDING FELLOW OF THE BRITISH ACADEMY
AUTHOR OF *RAILROAD TRANSPORTATION, ITS HISTORY AND LAWS*, &C., &C.

BEING LECTURES GIVEN AT BRITISH UNIVERSITIES
IN APRIL AND MAY, 1922, UNDER THE FOUNDATION
OF THE SIR GEORGE WATSON CHAIR OF AMERICAN
HISTORY, LITERATURE, AND INSTITUTIONS

CAMBRIDGE
AT THE UNIVERSITY PRESS
1923

CAMBRIDGE
UNIVERSITY PRESS

University Printing House, Cambridge CB2 8BS, United Kingdom

Published in the United States of America by Cambridge University Press, New York

Cambridge University Press is part of the University of Cambridge.

It furthers the University's mission by disseminating knowledge in the pursuit of education, learning and research at the highest international levels of excellence.

www.cambridge.org
Information on this title: www.cambridge.org/9781107683273

© Cambridge University Press 1923

First published 1923
First paperback edition 2014

A catalogue record for this publication is available from the British Library

ISBN 978-1-107-68327-3 Paperback

PREFATORY NOTE

BY THE SECRETARY

OF THE ANGLO-AMERICAN SOCIETY

THE INAUGURAL LECTURE UNDER the Foundation of the Sir George Watson Chair of American History, Literature, and Institutions (which is administered by the Anglo-American Society) was delivered by the late Viscount Bryce in 1921. His subject was "The Study of American History," and the lecture was subsequently published, towards the close of the same year, by the Cambridge University Press. For a full account of the origin of the Watson Chair readers are referred to the Appendix of that volume[1].

The present volume contains the first full course of lectures under the Watson Chair Foundation. They were delivered, in the spring of 1922, at London, Birmingham, Manchester, Sheffield, Cambridge, and Oxford, by Dr A. T. Hadley, President-Emeritus of Yale University, to large and representative audiences.

Dr Hadley has not only been, for more than twenty years, head of a great American university—he has

[1] *The Study of American History*, by Viscount Bryce, O.M., Cambridge, at the University Press, 1921, 3s. 6d. net.

also won practical experience of affairs as a director of a bank and of two railroad systems. The Anglo-American Society consider themselves fortunate to have secured the services of so eminent and representative an American scholar for the first course of lectures under the Watson Chair Foundation. They wish also to express their warm acknowledgments of the courtesy and kindness with which Dr Hadley was welcomed at the various British universities where his lectures were delivered.

H. S. PERRIS.

OFFICES OF THE ANGLO-AMERICAN SOCIETY,
    I CENTRAL BUILDINGS, LONDON, S.W. I.

CONTENTS

DEMOCRACIES OLD AND NEW

IN his recent book on *Modern Democracies*, my
honoured predecessor in this chair, Lord Bryce,
has set forth the workings of the machinery of popular
government in different countries so clearly and so
impartially as to leave little for others to add or
amend. I shall not have the temerity to follow in his
path, and try to travel again over ground which he
has so admirably covered, but shall approach the subject from a different angle; examining the various
industrial problems, national and international, by
which we are confronted at the present day, and
considering what measure of success in solving these
problems has attended the efforts of modern democratic governments in general and of the United
States of America in particular. Instead of making
the constitutional systems the primary object of our
enquiry, and the work of national housekeeping—
which is simply the English for Political Economy
—an incidental one, we shall take the housekeeping
problems first in order, and the methods of dealing
with them second.

This mode of studying democracy may not only
give us a somewhat novel viewpoint, but also serve to
promote, in a very important manner, that mutual

comprehension between our two countries which constitutes the primary object of the Watson Lectureship. There is no way in which two men get to understand one another more quickly than by comparing notes as to how they have met the same difficulties and perplexities under slightly different conditions. What is true of men individually seems likely to be true of nations. The industrial problems of Great Britain and the United States are similar in their general outlines. The difficulties which we meet and the perplexities under which we suffer in trying to solve them are almost identical. We can surely understand one another's politics better, and make more sympathetic allowance for their imperfection, if we look upon our governments as agencies which have grown up for dealing with common tasks and common ends, rather than as organisms which have developed separately and are maintained for their own separate purposes.

And besides helping us to understand one another, this way of looking at things may give us a better understanding of modern history as a whole.

All kinds of reasons have been given for the difference between ancient and modern history—between the old world of Greece and Rome and the present world of England and France and Germany and America. Some say that the distinction lay primarily in the *size* of the units involved; that Sparta and Athens, Carthage and Rome, were cities rather than nations, and that their whole political history bears the impress of this circumstance. Others attribute it to the fact that the line of cleavage in early days was one of religion rather than of race; that State and Church were far more closely united in the ancient world than they are in the modern; and that the bitterness of political contests, whether between different governments or between different elements in the same government, was intensified and prolonged by difference of religious tradition.

There is something to be said in favour of each of these views. Political units were undoubtedly smaller in the ancient world than they are in the modern. Religious kinship aroused more political enthusiasm then than it does now, and racial kinship less. But I think we have made more of these distinctions than the facts warrant. It is not right to say that the civilized world in the thousand years before the Christian era was made up of city-states in the same manner that the civilized world of today is made up of nations. This generalization is true as regards Greece and her colonies during the greater part of the period in question; and we know so much more about the history of Greece during these thousand years than we do about any other nation that we are apt to assume that it must have been true everywhere. But it cannot be made without reserve of any region except Greece. It was only partly true of Italy or of Phoenicia; it was not at all true of Egypt or of Persia. It cannot serve as a *general* explanation of the difference between ancient and modern statecraft.

Nor are we warranted in saying that the close connection between religion and politics was the dominant factor in making the history of the period which preceded the Christian era a different thing from what history is today. Then as now there were some states which emphasized the need of religious conformity as a basis of political equality, and some which ignored it. It is undoubtedly true that priestly offices and civil offices were more closely connected in the ancient world than in the modern; but it would be very hard indeed to prove that differences of religious opinion caused more wars or influenced internal politics more profoundly in old times than in new ones.

The thing that does distinguish modern history from ancient history is the decisive importance of industrial movements and industrial successes in determining the fate of nations. Conflicts which in old times were decided by superiority in military skill and personal courage are now decided by superior power to utilize the technical results of modern science and to organize the service of supply. In the modern struggle for existence between different races and different ideals, the centre of combat has shifted.

It is not the stronger race that wins, but the more provident race. It is not the readiness of its members to die for their country that makes a modern nation unconquerable so much as their readiness to work for their country.

This involves a radical change in the whole conception of the state. Whatever else a community does or does not do, it must be able to protect itself against foreign invasion or domination. For this purpose a trained soldiery is a necessary instrument; and in ancient times it was an all-sufficient instrument. If your army was superior to that of your rival in courage and in tactics, all other matters would take care of themselves. Industrial success followed military success almost of necessity. The victorious army lived on the enemy's country during the war in such a way as to reduce the national burdens to a minimum; and at the end of the war it brought booty and tribute to increase its country's present wealth, and slaves to maintain its future productiveness.

These facts were accepted as a matter of course and formed the basis of the morals and politics of the ancient world. Slavery was an unchallenged institution. A few advanced thinkers urged that Greeks should not make slaves of their fellow Greeks from rival cities; but when a Spartan commander proposed to put this theory into practice, the general comment

was "*C'est magnifique mais ce n'est pas la guerre.*" The
constitution of the Greek States centred about the
army. Politically the body of soldiers, actual or
potential, was the *demos* or people. The question
which occupied the minds of writers like Aristotle
was whether political authority and office should be
divided as equally as possible among the whole body
of soldiers, or whether men of family and wealth
should be given a preferential position. And even
where preference was given to men of wealth it was
not because the management of property had fitted
them for service in the state; it was because the mere
possession of such property was an assurance of the
conservative spirit which a purely democratic government was so apt to lack.

We know less about the politics of other ancient
races than we do about those of the Greeks; but there
is every reason to believe that the Greek experience,
as described by Herodotus or Thucydides and summarized by Aristotle, was typical of what befell every
civilized or semi-civilized state in the Mediterranean
group during the eight centuries that preceded the
Christian era, and left its impress upon the politics
of the Roman Empires, old and new, during the
thirteen centuries that followed it. Power and privilege confined to members of the army and distributed
among various ranks according to their relative
military efficiency under the particular form of tactics

which prevailed at the moment; a perpetual balancing between the danger of revolution if too little influence was accorded to the common soldiers, and the danger of capricious government and resulting weakness if too much influence was accorded them; land tenure based upon military occupancy, and arranged primarily to serve the needs of public security rather than those of agricultural productiveness; industry, other than farming, controlled by aliens, and labour performed by slaves—these were the characteristics of the ancient state, whether it called itself an aristocracy or a democracy.

Under these circumstances the importance of economic efficiency as a factor in national strength and international politics remained unnoticed to an amazing degree. At a time when the industrial arts were carried to the very highest pitch as a means of private and public adornment or luxury, industrial science developed but slowly, and its possible bearing on national defence was neglected or misunderstood. Wars were lost and won without much assistance from the inventor or the property owner—except as the property owner paid part of the immediate cost in taxes. When we consider how large a part of the time of the ancient world was devoted to fighting, the most astonishing thing about ancient warfare is its unprogressiveness. In the many centuries which elapsed between the invention of bronze armour and the military utilization of gunpowder there was no fundamental change in military methods. Cavalry gave place to infantry and close fighting to open fighting, or *vice versa*, according to peculiarities of terrain or temperament. Men gradually learned to forge better armour, build stronger walls and manage larger ships. But there was less actual progress in a millennium than there now is in a decade. The armies of Charlemagne would have had no such advantage over the Roman legions or the Macedonian phalanxes as the regiments of today have over those of ten years ago.

It is easy to see why soldiers trained in this school and statesmen dominated by its traditions would regard surplus production of wealth above the immediate necessities of the commonwealth as likely to cause national weakness rather than strength. If distributed as largess it was demoralizing; if not distributed, but stored up, it invited hostility from lawless men within the community, or lawless communities whose lands adjoined it. The industrial wealth of Egypt 500 years before the Christian era or of Rome 500 years after it, proved more potent as a temptation to attack than as a means of defence.

A brief history of the causes which gradually attracted the attention of soldiers and statesmen to the importance of organized industry may not be out of place.

Shortly after the invention of firearms, and largely in consequence of new tactical methods which followed that invention, armies of the modern type, regularly officered and supplied, proved their superiority both to the large irregular levies of partly trained troops on which England or France had previously relied and to the well trained but comparatively small groups of *condottieri* or mercenaries on whom Italian sovereigns were apt to depend. War had become too continuous a business for the former, and too big a business for the latter. In the effective utilization of a considerable army equipped with firearms the problem of supply assumed dominant importance. To maintain continuous pressure on the enemy abroad it became necessary to provide stores of food and of munitions at home. The productiveness of a nation's land became a vital factor in the struggle for existence. The old feudal land tenures which were based on military considerations now gradually gave place to other forms of tenure calculated to secure the economic surplus necessary as a basis for effective fighting under modern conditions. The history of this change is very complex, and its outcome differed in different countries. England developed the capitalist-landlord, France the peasant-proprietor, Italy the system of share-rents. But in every one of these countries the "servile" tenures which were so habitual down to the thirteenth century had given place by the eighteenth century to a system of land-holdings which made owner and occupier largely independent of feudal authority even in countries whose political constitution had remained wholly undemocratic.

When the surplus product of the land under this new system was not used up in war, it became available as *capital*. The owner could use it as a help to future production; thereby securing advantage both for himself and for the community. Of course there were many instances where mistakes were made, and where the growth of surplus wealth proved a source of weakness rather than of strength; but in the long run, the governments that encouraged investment of capital were rewarded by a decided accession of power both in peace and in war. For where capital was abundant, there was always an increased number of mechanical aids to production and trade which made labour more efficient; and there was apt to be an increase in the spirit of invention and the opportunities given the inventor, so that new methods of working and of fighting could be rapidly developed. That these changes met national needs is shown by the history of the laws regarding prices and interest rates from the thirteenth century to the seventeenth.

Prior to the thirteenth century, moralists and lawyers had been content to accept Aristotle's *dictum* that the value or just price of an article was proportionate to the labour expended in producing it; that any charge in excess of this was unfair; and that the attempt to make an interest charge on capital loaned to the producer, however much he might need it to increase the efficiency of his labour, was a conspicuous instance of such unfairness. Now in the time of Aristotle, when practically all labour was slave labour, and when borrowed money could seldom be so used as to increase the borrower's ability to pay, this view was probably right enough in practice. An hour of slave labour in one line is about as valuable as an hour of slave labour in another line. A dollar or a pound today is about as useful to one as a dollar or a pound six months hence. But when we are dealing with free labour, or with capital invested in business, the case is entirely altered. One man's labour is worth a great deal more than another man's; capital today may be worth more than capital tomorrow; it is to the eternal credit of English judges that they perceived this alteration so promptly. The only possible criterion of the value of an article in such cases is the amount the buyers are willing to pay; and if the resulting profit is higher in some cases than others, the best way to remedy the disproportion is to encourage the investment of capital in the lines where products are wanted in order that the price may be reduced by competition. The underlying good sense of this view was so obvious that it gradually became a principle of modern law, Roman as well as English. Occasional attempts to revert to Aristotle's theories as a basis of social justice have simply resulted in a reversion to Aristotle's conditions—uniform inefficiency of labour and virtual disappearance of capital. No better illustration can be asked than that of Russia during the last four years.

Out of this complex of causes was born a different world, and a different social order, from any that had previously been dreamed of; a world whose fundamental problems had ceased to be military and were becoming industrial; a social order still administered under principles derived from Roman lawyers, but animated by public purposes and shaped by public needs of which Rome knew nothing. Only within the last fifty years have we seen the full meaning of the change from feudalism to industrialism, or the full difficulty of the problems which modern democracy has to face. And even today, with the changed conditions fully before us, we scarcely understand how different is the position and the task of the modern state, and particularly of the modern democracy, from that of *any* ancient state, however free or enlightened. We appreciate in a general way that the vitality of a modern nation is primarily a matter of industrial strength and soundness even more than of military strength and soundness; but we fail to realize in any specific way how many questions, unknown to statesmen of earlier ages, are involved in the maintenance of that strength and soundness.

We have to take constant care not to be misled by similarity of names and definitions. The Athenian democracy, like the American democracy, was a "government by the citizens at large"—or in modern phrase a government whose political power was shared with approximate equality by all men who possessed full civil rights. The old democracy and the new had many external points of similarity. They also had one internal danger in common—the danger that government by the citizens at large would degenerate from a constitutional republic or commonwealth administered in the interest of the state as a whole to an unchecked rule of the majority exercised for the benefit of the poor at the expense of the rich. Much of what Aristotle says on this last point applies with but slight change to the political history and political experience of the nineteenth century. But here the resemblance ends. When we enquire what was meant by the citizens at large, or what problems they were called upon to discuss, we find ourselves in a different world from our own. To Aristotle or any other Athenian the admission of labourers or artisans to full civil rights was unthinkable. If I may borrow a metaphor from athletics which applies very closely and subtly, they did not possess the necessary "amateur standing." Under these circumstances their exclusion from political power even in the freest democracies followed as a matter of course. The industrial population of the Athenian state, constituting probably three-fifths of the whole, had no chance to take part in public affairs in any way. The really difficult problems of today—the labour problem, the race problem, the population problem— were not political problems at all to the Athenian or to the citizens of any other ancient state. They might take the form of public dangers; but even in that case they did not arouse political controversies or animosities. They led the citizens to drop such controversies in the pressure of a common peril, and to unite in the defence of their own privileges as a superior caste.

Here lies the great practical difference between government by the people in Greece or Rome or medieval Switzerland on the one hand and in England or America on the other. The Greek or Roman or Swiss Commonwealth was confronted by a comparatively simple task. It had to keep itself in readiness for war and to hold the balance between different groups in a military caste in such a way as to prevent internal disorders. This was practically all. The burden of the modern democracy is heavier. It must keep itself, by its technique and organization, as far to the front as possible in the industrial race. It must

also get the hard and disagreeable work of industry
done by men who are voters; and secure the consent
of these voters to some system which will provide
the accumulations of capital and the centralized control by far-sighted men of business which are necessary conditions of modern progress.

The task of the ancient state was not only a simple
one, it was one in which democracy could work
with special advantage. For, contrary to the popular
opinion, democracy shows at its best in fighting, and
particularly in 'old-fashioned fighting. The world has
a long record of amazing defeats of large monarchies
by small republics which were apparently much
weaker. Xerxes against Athens, Charles of Burgundy
against Switzerland or Philip of Spain against the
Netherlands are typical instances. Defeats of a republic by a monarchy are comparatively rare; defeats
of a large republic by a small monarchy are practically
unknown.

Nor should this be a matter of wonder. Democracy
if kept in any sort of control tends to develop many
of the qualities which are essential to the *morale* of
an army. Men fight more tenaciously when they
fight for something which they and their fathers have
built up. They rise to emergencies better if they have
been trained in the habit of self-government. The
fighting efficiency of a democracy is on the whole less
dependent on the continuous success of its generals

than is the case with a monarchy. So far as we can judge from the somewhat partisan accounts which have come down to us, the wars of the Roman Republic began with defeats almost as often as with victories; but in the long run the *morale* of the Roman army and of the republic behind it counted for more in determining the issue than the generalship of Pyrrhus or of Hannibal.

Military aristocracies in all ages have made the mistake of thinking that people who had been trained to judge for themselves and act for their own interest would not submit to authority readily enough to form a disciplined army. But the pressure of national peril, and the fear of foreign domination make the whole body of citizens see that their country's interest is their own interest. If a man voluntarily and wholeheartedly submits himself to discipline on this ground, the fact that he has been trained in habits of self-government and self-command adds to his efficiency instead of subtracting from it. This is why democracy has been seen at its best in war. This is why democratic states have so often beaten monarchies whose armies were better commanded and better equipped. But it is a question—and for the lovers of freedom a very grave question—how far this advantage of democracy will continue if war itself becomes an industrial problem to be solved by superior preparation in chemistry or in economics, instead of a contest to be won by superior courage and intelligence in an emergency.

The constant peril of democracy in the modern industrial state is that it may not be able to secure the same unselfishness and the same voluntary subordination of the individual interest to the public interest in times of peace as it can in times of war. A free people will rise to meet emergencies; but can it be trusted to foresee them and prepare for them? Will the great body of citizens work that others may accumulate? Will they in ordinary times accept the counsel of far-seeing statesmen or scientific experts on matters in which they themselves are less competent to judge? Can we secure the pleasures and advantages of liberty and the industrial progress that has gone with it without exposing ourselves to the perils of internal conflict between hand-workers and brain-workers that so often attend it? Can we develop an industrial *morale* which shall serve the commonwealth in times of peace as effectively as its military *morale* has served it in times of war? This was the really critical point in the problem which confronted the constituent assemblies of America and of France in the closing years of the eighteenth century; in the problem with which each English colony has had to deal when it grew up to industrial manhood; in the problem which has been more and more insistently brought home to England herself with every

accession of strength to the democratic elements in
her constitution.

It took thoughtful democrats some time to recognize the importance, or even the existence, of
this element in the situation. The members of the
American constitutional convention of 1788 or the
French national assembly of 1789 were so busy in
guarding against past evils and dangers, with which
history had rendered them familiar, that they had
little time to spare for considering future perils that
could only be surmised. The dangers in times past
had come from three directions. Sometimes the
arbitrary authority of a monarch had been strong
enough to defy the popular will and set popular
liberties at naught. Sometimes an aristocracy had
been able to maintain special privileges which rendered
political equality impossible. Sometimes the people
itself was so much divided that the central government was too weak to meet collective needs of national
defence or national unity. These were difficulties of
the kind which could be largely if not wholly cured
by good constitutional machinery; and statesmen like
Hamilton or Jefferson in America and Mirabeau or
Sieyès in France, set themselves to work to devise
the best machinery they could. To hold the different
parts together they relied on the system of representative assemblies. To prevent the executive officers of
the government from using their power in defiance

of popular will or disregard of popular liberty, they gave their representative assemblies powers of control similar to those possessed by the English Parliament —as this had in times past proved the best of all the means provided by large nations for checking the arbitrary authority of monarchs. To prevent the abuse of special privileges by an aristocracy they abolished the outward marks and legal incidents of privilege altogether. *La carrière ouverte aux talents* was made a fundamental principle of public law.

Judged as a piece of machinery the work of the American constitution makers was remarkably good; and, judged by the same standard, the work of the French national assembly probably deserves a more favourable verdict than it has generally received. The internal conditions of France had been so bad, and the experience of her people in self-government had been so small, that any movement in the direction of freedom was sure to be attended by a great deal of violence and many backward steps. The thing that prevented the first French Republic from meeting the legitimate demands of the French people, and that has prevented the American Republic from fully realizing the ideals of some of its founders regarding liberty or equality, lies deeper than any mere defect of machinery. The extent to which democracy can be carried depends more upon national education than upon constitutional law.

Few of the founders of modern democracy saw this at all clearly. The thing which seemed important to them was that the government should carefully represent and conscientiously carry out the popular will. They did not see how often the majority which was supposed to express that popular will was imperfectly educated regarding the facts at issue, and therefore at once short-sighted and selfish in its demands. Still less did they understand the *increasing* strain which democracy was going to put upon popular intelligence and self-subordination. If the old democracies had enough of these qualities to serve in times of war they thought that the modern democracies would have enough to serve in times of peace. They did not know how much harder the industrial problem was than the military one, nor how rapidly its difficulties were going to increase in the years that have elapsed since 1789.

Our central problem today, even more than in 1789, is one of education—how to train a free people to *work* voluntarily, side by side and yet with due subordination, in the same way that Greece and Italy trained free peoples to *fight* voluntarily side by side and with due subordination. What an industrial democracy can do today depends on its past training in these qualities; what advances it can make tomorrow will depend upon its capacity to receive further training. The success of a commonwealth

rests not so much on its natural advantages, or on
its legal machinery, as on the political intelligence of
its citizens. Its statesmen must use applied psychology quite as often as applied economics. They have
to decide not only what is best for the nation under
given circumstances, but how and when the people—
or a majority of the people—can be made to see that
it *is* best. An American political leader may be able
to prove to his own satisfaction that the attempt to
collect the debts which allied governments owe to
his country will cripple its prospective trade with
other nations; but how far can he bring its argument
home to those who do not understand the principles
of foreign exchange, or to those who fear the competition of foreign labour in their own industries
more than they value the opportunity to buy and sell
in foreign markets? To accomplish anything substantial he must be able to enlist either the self-
interest or the public spirit of an organized majority
to support him in getting measures passed and con-
sidered. The question whether a monarchy has free-
trade or protection, inflation or deflation, private
railway ownership or government railway ownership,
may be decided by convincing one man who identifies
(or may be supposed to identify) the public interest
with his own. In a democracy the decision of each
of these questions may involve an appeal to millions
of voters with many of whom the apparent conflict

between their own individual interests and those of the commonwealth is very strong.

When the revolution of 1917 made Russia a democracy, it was easy for students of economics or of history to see that the proposals of Miliukoff were wiser than those of Kerensky, and that those of Kerensky were wiser than those of Lenin. But the matter was not to be settled by the intrinsic wisdom of the proposals, but by the judgment of the Russian people. This was a logical and necessary consequence of the fact that Russia was a democracy. And the Russian people, being inexperienced in economics and in history, accepted Lenin instead of Miliukoff or Kerensky, in the same way that the French people, a century and a quarter before, preferred Robespierre to La Fayette or Vergniaud, and paid the same penalty.

This is simply an extreme illustration of what may happen in any popular government. Every statesman sees that each economic problem which comes before him is in the large sense an educational one; that the particular form in which his difficulties come up is determined by the past training which the people have had, and that their acceptance of his solution depends, not on the intrinsic soundness of his arguments alone, but on the popular ability to understand them and readiness to act upon them. It is the appreciation of this fact which distinguishes the statesman from the *doctrinaire*.

The intelligent citizens of each country know something of the difficulties by which their own statesmen are confronted. An Englishman may agree with Lloyd George or may disagree with him, but in either event he understands the limitations under which Lloyd George works better than he understands those which have hampered Briand or Poincaré in France, and Wilson or Harding in America; and he is in perpetual danger of thinking that foreign statesmen fail to see what they ought to do, when they simply cannot make their fellow citizens see it. We in America are correspondingly ill-informed about the conditions which confront Lloyd George, and are in constant danger of misjudging him on that account. I believe that this is what causes a large part of the misunderstanding between intelligent members of different nations—as distinct from the unintelligent manifestation of racial prejudice or racial animosity. Each people is able to make proper allowance for the difficulties under which its own statesmen work, and cannot make similar allowance for the statesmen of other countries, but thinks that they ought to be guided by abstract principles of economic expediency or justice. It has a double standard of judgment; a theoretical one for others, a practical one for itself. And such double standards are always perilous.

If this is true, I am sure I shall contribute most to the understanding between our two great countries if I treat the economic problems in which we are both concerned as being also educational problems, and show how their present form and their possible solution are dependent on the nation's character and have been determined by the past history of each people. I shall lay comparatively little stress on the momentary phases and incidents of our race problem or our labour problem or our railroad problem; I shall speak rather of the conditions which determine the attitude of our citizens as a body toward these various problems. It is with the background of the scene that I am concerned, more than with the foreground—the background which changes but slowly, however fast the scenes may shift.

Most publicists have paid scant attention to this background. They have been more concerned with developing free institutions than with developing habits of self-government; they have trusted the solution of the nation's business problems to the enlightened self-interest of the individual, without realizing what kind and what degree of enlightenment was necessary in order to get them solved by that means. And the main problem of democracy in the twentieth century—the fundamental problem in England and in America, no less than in Continental Europe—is to secure this kind of enlightenment before it is too late.

I do not mean that nineteenth century commonwealths have neglected public education, but that they have failed to see what kind of education was needed by the citizens of a democracy in order to keep the commonwealth industrially strong, both against outside enemies and against internal strife. They have spent constantly increasing sums upon their school systems and have put opportunities of acquiring knowledge within the reach of all to an extent which was undreamed of a few years ago. But the acquisition of knowledge is only a part of education, and not the largest or most important part. The chief end of training, in the schools and in after life, is the development of habits and powers and ideals—habits of discipline and of self-command, powers of hard and efficient work, ideals of duty which will lead a man to sacrifice present enjoyment for future honour and personal profit for public service. We must train not only intelligent individuals, but useful citizens.

Ancient democracies have given ample recognition to the importance of this public end in education. Plato and Aristotle are full of discussions concerning the training of the citizen—the methods of teaching, in school and in after life, which would develop the qualities needed by the freeman in a commonwealth like Athens. Modern monarchies like Prussia have learned the lesson taught by Plato and Aristotle in regard to the importance of the political aim in education. The schools, the army and the church of northern Germany during the last half-century were treated as coördinated parts of an educational system which taught the virtues of the subject as consistently as Athens ever tried to teach those of the freeman. Devotion to national ideals and voluntary subordination to monarchical authority combined with habits of hard work and marvellous technical efficiency—these were the carefully planned results of Prussian teaching. The faults through which Germany lost the war were due to defects in the vision of the Hohenzollerns themselves, rather than to any failure to train the German people to realize that vision.

The Hohenzollerns failed in their plans of conquest from the same defect which has so often caused the plans of monarchs in earlier ages to miscarry—a lack of understanding of the character and feelings of their neighbours. They forgot that the maxim "The king can do no wrong" holds good only within each king's own frontiers, and that beyond them he must expect to be judged by the same standards as any other man. They were genuinely surprised when methods of waging war which would have frightened their own subjects into submission drove the citizens of neighbouring commonwealths into fiercer resistance, or when neutrals refused to accord to German official documents the same ready credence which was given them at home, and insisted upon judging the acts of the Emperor's government by their own rules of evidence and their own standards of international morality. As a result of this blindness Germany made a succession of mistakes which united against her a group of nations strong enough to overcome whatever initial advantage she had won by her preparations for war and her unscrupulousness in using them. But the contest was so close, and the peril to which the Allies were exposed was so grave, that we may well pause to consider whether the educational systems of our great modern republics have been up to the standard of present-day requirements—whether they are as good for our purposes as were those of Germany for her purposes.

And the answer is by no means reassuring. In America, at any rate, the public purpose in education has been allowed to fall into the background. We have been more concerned in recent years to make teaching in our schools agreeable to the pupil than to inculcate habits of hard work and self-subordination which shall be useful to the state. We have secured tolerably good discipline, but inadequate self-reliance and technical efficiency. We have developed general ideals of patriotism which were effective in time of war; but we have not learned to subordinate individual demands to national needs in time of peace. In some cases, the bad effect of free public high schools in teaching the pupils to expect the government to give them something for nothing appears to have out-weighed the value of the knowledge they have imparted.

Such is the educational balance-sheet of America today; and though the individual items might read differently in England or in her colonies, I suspect that the mixture of good and bad assets would be in about the same proportion. And a similar mixture of good and bad assets, of adequacy and inadequacy, will be seen when we turn our attention to the training which the citizen receives in after life, in present-day business and present-day politics. I am planning to do this in subsequent lectures; and I think that we shall everywhere be impressed with the conclusion that existing industrial conditions cannot be met except by securing greater political intelligence and greater public spirit, and shaping our laws and institutions to that end. Every great economic problem of today is fundamentally an educational one. The question how to train the people to meet the conditions which confront them is even more important than the question how to arrange the conditions to meet the demands of the people.

ECONOMIC FREEDOM

THE democrats of the eighteenth century had a whole-hearted belief in individual liberty, quite different from anything which characterizes their successors in the twentieth. They held with Rousseau that most of the natural impulses of the human mind were right ones and that nine-tenths of all our political and social evils arose from the unwise efforts of the few to restrict the freedom of the many. All that they asked of any government was a sufficient control over the actions of the wicked minority to prevent them from interfering with the good men who constituted the majority. If this were secured, the self-interest of each individual would lead him to work hard in order to acquire property, and to produce the things which the community demanded. So they reasoned; and Adam Smith's great work, *The Wealth of Nations*, which appeared in the same year as the Declaration of Independence of the United States, seemed to confirm the soundness of their reasoning. To men who held these views, property seemed a natural right, almost as much as liberty; and in some of the earlier manifestos of the French Revolution it was actually so described.

The one place where the democrats of the old

school really had a chance to try out these views was
the United States of America.   For this was the only
country where the merits and defects of democracy
in dealing with modern industrial conditions were at
all fully tested in the first half of the nineteenth
century. The colonies of Great Britain had not received full rights of self-government. The republics
of South America found quite enough to do in maintaining their own existence without attempting to
solve industrial problems. Even in Switzerland the
position and authority of the Federal Government was
not placed on a permanent or definite basis till 1848.

The problem which lay before the American
Commonwealth in 1789 was in many respects a unique
one. Other federations had been charged with the
duty of making a nation out of elements that already
existed. This one had to create the elements as well
as to unite them. The territory of which the United
States found herself in possession at that time was
underpopulated to an extraordinary degree. Never in
the recent history of the world has so large and fertile
a domain supported so small a population as was the
case in North America under the dominion of the
Indians. They were so backward in industry that
they could neither multiply their own numbers nor
amalgamate with the more productive races; while at
the same time they were so forward in the arts of war
that they had contrived to exterminate all the higher

civilizations with which they had come in contact until the advent of the white men from Europe. Under these circumstances the country presented a clean sheet on which the statesman gifted with industrial knowledge and industrial vision might write what he pleased.

Other nations have always been face to face with the question how they should make their land support their population. The United States during the first century of her existence had the opposite question: how to secure a population which should occupy and utilize the land. Natural resources were abundant; labour was scarce. How should she get this labour? She might of course have trusted to the natural increase of her own numbers. But this policy would have involved private loss and public danger. As a matter of private business, it would have prevented the cultivator from making the profit of which he foresaw the possibilities if he had labour to develop the resources that lay before him. And it would have had this public danger: that, by leaving the western land unutilized, it would have led the English to send colonists up the St Lawrence, and the Spaniards or French to send them up the Mississippi, in such numbers that the United States would soon find the back country taken out of her hands and the most fertile parts of the continent occupied by alien, if not hostile, powers. It was vitally necessary for America to attract immigration, and to find means by which the immigrants could be made competent citizens of a self-governing community.

Washington's great Secretary of the Treasury, Alexander Hamilton, saw the possibility of utilizing the public domain for these purposes. This domain was very large. Except for a fringe along the Atlantic Ocean, which belonged to the thirteen chartered colonies of England and constituted only a small fraction of the whole, the unsettled land of the United States was the public property of the national government. Some of the colonies had had claims to parts of this western territory; but when the Constitution was formed in 1789 they ceded these rights to the national government, which thus became the undisputed owner of an area of several million square miles which it could use as it pleased. Hamilton laid down the principle, which was accepted at the time and never has been abandoned, that the public domain should not be used primarily for the profit of the government but should be administered with a view to the rapid settlement and sound development of the country as a whole. In pursuance of this policy, arrangements were made for the survey of the public lands at as early a date as possible. Survey lines were run at intervals of half a mile, both from north to south and from east to west, dividing the country into square sections of the area of a quarter of a mile, or

160 acres each. These are the "quarter sections" so constantly alluded to in the land laws of the United States. On the lands thus surveyed the standard price was first fixed at $2.00 an acre, but was afterwards reduced to $1.25. And this cheap rate was not the only inducement offered to settlers. By a series of "Preëmption Acts" from 1801 to 1841 a man who had actually settled upon public land but could not pay for it was given a priority claim to the land thus occupied. It was, in a sense, reserved for a time when he might be ready to purchase. Nobody could buy it over his head. The result of these Preëmption Acts was that a man could enter upon land and register his occupancy of it, with the assurance that he would benefit by the improvements which he made, and have a chance to buy the land itself out of the proceeds of his successful farming. And a still further step in the direction of encouraging the actual settlement of land was made by the passage of the "Homestead Act" in 1862, which virtually meant that if a man would cultivate land himself and make proper entries and affidavits for the Land Records he could get title to 160 acres at a merely nominal cost.

It took some time for the full effects of Hamilton's land policy to make themselves felt. Down to the year 1815 popular movements in Europe gave restless or ambitious spirits enough to do at home, without crossing the ocean to seek their fortunes. But after the close of the Napoleonic wars the situation was altered. Settlers came in rapidly increasing numbers. They found, not only that political equality which the laws had promised, but—on the frontier at any rate—an environment which gave men of intelligence and industry such chances for material and social advancement as the world had never seen. They became members of a community of workers, where each citizen was ready to accept as his equal anybody else who was ready to work hard—a community where an industrious man was far more respected than an idle one, and had a greater chance of obtaining honours and offices.

These early settlers on the American frontiers were labourers of much more than ordinary ability. They were picked men, who, on account of industrial or social ambition, had ventured to take a step which was then comparatively rare. The Atlantic Ocean in 1830 was not the casual summer resort which it has today become. It was a vast and appalling barrier, full of unknown terrors. A man who crossed it with his family had some very strong motive for doing so—and that motive was usually a good one. The majority of the immigrants were men of decided political capacity. They not only occupied the land, they trained themselves for citizenship while doing so. It was these Western settlers who created the

American type of character, and determined the course of American industrial history.

Colonization on the Atlantic coast had been predominantly English; and even after the separation of the colonies from the mother country the characteristics of their people and their society remained English for many years to come. The external signs of this resemblance were more obvious in the South than in the North; for the climate and soil of the South favoured the development of large estates tilled by slave labour and owned by devotees of outdoor sport. At the time of the Revolution the Southern colonies therefore had an aristocracy not unlike that of England in its habits, assumptions, and interests. But the North also had an aristocracy of its own, less given to outward show than that of the South, but not one whit less proud; an aristocracy of magistrates and ministers, brought up in the Puritan tradition to fear God and naught beside. The social system of the North was less rigid than that of the South; inheritance counted for less in determining a man's social position, and personal character and ability for more. But neither South nor North, in the closing years of the eighteenth century, possessed an industrial *democracy* or anything like it.

It was in the West that industrial democracy really started. Settlers from North and South, and immigrants from Europe in small but constantly increasing numbers, crossed the Alleghany Mountains into a country where they were equal before the law and pretty nearly equal in the face of nature—a country to which little material wealth could be transported and in most of which slave labour was unproductive or unavailable. Here was realized, more fully than had been possible in either the Northern or Southern colonies of England, that freedom and equality which the Declaration of American Independence characterized as the birthright of all men. What to the signers of the declaration had been a phrase to justify their independence of English rule— or at most a remote ideal which they did not expect to see realized—became at once a living, potent fact. A people grew up west of the Alleghany Mountains with whom social equality was a fundamental assumption; a people of self-reliant men and women, ready to work and take their chances of survival; a people whose philosophy is aptly summarized in Stephen Leacock's couplet:

> Thus does the race of man decay and rot;
> Some men can hold their jobs and some cannot!

Most of them were devout believers in the Christian religion and much attached to their own particular form of worship; but they were accustomed to judge men by what they did and not by what they professed. And this saved them from intolerance. They were enthusiastically devoted to their country and to its government; but they asked little of that government except that it should protect land titles and appoint honest judges. They were admirably fitted by temperament and training to carry the theory of free competition to its logical conclusion and reach the kind of result which Adam Smith or John Stuart Mill would have predicted.

This development of the West had an effect upon the East, which began to be felt about 1820, and increased rapidly as years went on. Almost every family in the states of the Atlantic seaboard had one or two members who had "gone West." These were apt to be among its strongest and most enterprising members; and their experience of this new environment modified the attitude of their relatives in regard to social questions. Particularly strong was this influence upon the younger generation who had grown up under American public law instead of English public law, and were ready to modify their social standards accordingly. The result was a change in the whole character of American politics, Eastern as well as Western. In the years prior to 1820 property qualifications for office, and even for the suffrage itself, had been quite generally imposed. Between 1820 and 1840 they were practically done away with. In the course of a great movement of which Andrew Jackson was the popular leader, the country became a democracy in fact as well as in name.

But social standards did not change so fast as political ones; and any alteration in this respect was much more difficult in the South than in the North. For the South was an aristocracy of large planters; while the North was an aristocracy of professional men, ship-owners and relatively small land-holders. Under Northern conditions there were no very sharp social lines to break down; and the older generation acquiesced in changes which they were powerless to prevent. In the South the case was different. The planters were strong enough to make a fight for the old system. They tried to meet the growth of free labour in the Northwest by the extension of slave labour in the Southwest. They added Texas and parts of Mexico to the national domain. They made several attempts to annex Cuba; they talked of reopening the slave trade. Under the masterly leadership of Mr Calhoun of South Carolina they retained a dominant influence in the politics of the nation long after they had become a minority in its numbers. Deprived of that leadership by his death in 1850 they soon lost political control and attempted to secede from the Union. This was a double mistake; first because it antagonized a large number of men in the North who had had no very great objection to slavery but were unwilling to have their country dismembered by act of a minority; and second because a belligerent that depends on slave labour for its industrial basis is in no condition to carry on a long war against one which can command free labour. The South fought magnificently and was well led; but in a war of attrition, economic superiority was bound to be the decisive factor. The war ended with an almost unresisted sweep of the Northern armies over an industrially exhausted South. The triumph of the Western ideal was complete. The United States between 1860 and 1865 ceased to be a confederation of two different kinds of republics and became a true democracy, in the modern sense of the word; a place where there is substantial equality of civil and political rights among all qualified members of the community.

The American nation, having thus found the way to get its land settled by a self-reliant and hard-working population whose ideals conformed to those of the Constitution and public law of the land, had a further problem to consider—that of securing the necessary capital. One form of capital, and only one, it possessed in abundance—surplus food. The returns from the land were so great that there was no shortage in this respect, except from unforeseen local causes like floods or fires. But it had no stock of accumulated wealth in forms which could render production and exchange more efficient or consumption more diversified.

To make good this deficiency in capital it was ready to adopt almost every means that political economists would approve, and quite a number that they would not approve. To encourage investment, high rates of interest were paid by the people, and permitted by the public authorities. If usury laws stood on the statute books they were tacitly ignored or evaded. When capital invested in farms or mills or mines would yield from fifteen to twenty per cent., it was obvious folly to balk at paying ten or twelve per cent. interest. The right of incorporation was likewise bestowed with the utmost freedom. When a whole community wanted railroads and factories it seemed suicidal to burden the promoters with the duty of proving that they met a public necessity, or even that they were quite correct in all their arrangements for securing solvency. The typical Western settler was incurably optimistic—otherwise he would hardly have gone West—and looked more to the needs of today than to those of tomorrow. He knew that his community needed a railroad or a factory; as to the future of that railroad or factory he was quite content to trust in the Lord.

This laxity in the law of incorporation was promoted by the federal system under which the United States is governed. There are two important differences of method between America and England in the public regulation of business affairs. One is that most of this regulation in America is done by state law instead of by national law as in England. The other is that many things like railway charters which in England would be made the subject of private bills or acts of Parliament, in America are regulated by general statutes of the particular state or states concerned. Now in the years from 1830 to 1870 there was a great deal of rivalry between the newer states of the Union in getting streams of capital from the seaboard and from Europe to flow in their direction. The competition between individual concerns in offering high rates of interest was accompanied and reinforced by a competition between different state legislatures in making laws which allowed favourable—not to say loose—methods of incorporation.

An extreme example of this laxity was shown in the early history of American banking. Like all new communities, the Western states and territories of the Union in the early part of the nineteenth century suffered from habitual deficiency of cash. Where roads and buildings and machinery are so much needed and money invested in these forms yields such large returns in the way of profit to the individual and of advantage to the community, not only is the individual always short of ready money, but the banks are constantly tempted to reduce their gold reserve below the point of safety. It is easy to see that any such course on the part of the banks must be disastrous in the long run. But neither Western business men nor Western legislatures were looking very far ahead. They were not so much concerned about keeping banks solvent as about having banks started; not so much interested in the problem of getting currency redeemed as in the problem of getting it issued. During the early years of the Republic the Democratic party opposed federal banks not simply on constitutional grounds, but also because their conservatism in issuing notes was regarded as a reflection on the more patriotic policy of state banks in furnishing their respective communities with all the money they desired. Intimations were not wanting that the national bank was a device of the wealthy foreigner and his confederates to prevent the poor American from getting as rich as he ought to.

It is significant of the spirit of the times that amid all this demand for free banking there was no desire for issue of government notes with forced circulation. People's distrust of government was stronger than their love of paper money. They were ready to take doubtful paper of their own free will; they were not ready to have government assume the responsibility for it or compel others to take it. The possibility of loss they were ready to stand; but they would not stand the possibility of interference with their own liberty and that of their fellow men which the issue of government paper seemed to involve.

There were one or two groups of cases, however, in which this desire for capital overcame their distrust of government action. The country's need of means of communication was so great that grants of public land to canal companies and railway companies were quite universally popular. Even those who most distrusted the government and all its works, and felt with Tom Paine that "society arose from men's wants, government from their wickedness," could see little harm in allowing the government to give away something that nobody was using, to somebody who would, or at least might, use it to meet a public demand. And there was also a sentiment, less universal but still very considerable, in favour of some protection to infant industries—arising not so much from any belief in the theories of protection as now enunciated, as from a patriotic desire of each town to have mills and the diversity of local industry that goes with them; and from a belief that a protective tariff, under the conditions then existing in America, would hasten this result.

In spite of this leaning toward protection, it was in surroundings like these, and among men like these, that the economic principle of competition and the political maxim of *laissez-faire* had their fullest development and showed most completely their possibilities in the way of good or of evil. It was here that the assumptions of Adam Smith or John Stuart Mill regarding the intelligent pursuit of self-interest by each individual were most nearly realized. Those of us who were brought up on the old-fashioned text-books of political economy can hardly conceive how small a part of the prices or wages or rents of the world has actually been determined by competition. It is only in the wholesale markets for commodities, and particularly for those commodities where there is a good deal of international trade, that competition can be treated as the one dominant influence compared with which all other factors in determining price are negligible.

Retail prices in most countries and most ages are determined by custom rather than by competition. If the wholesale price of an article goes down, the consumers seldom know it promptly and still more seldom get much advantage from it. Even if there is no actual combination among the retailers of a given district, most retailers find it easier to keep on selling to their old customers at the old rate rather than to seek new customers at lower rates. And if the wholesale price of an article goes up, the buyers object so actively to any corresponding advance in the cost to them, that the retailer will often forfeit a large part of his normal profit rather than incur a reputation as an extortioner. If the scarcity which has raised the wholesale price continues for a long time, corresponding changes in the retail price must follow: but these changes are usually rather slow.

What is so often true of retail prices is still more generally true of wages. It is only by a stretch of the imagination that we can speak of an English labour market or a French labour market. Walter Bagehot pointed out long ago that the English labourer could not move rapidly enough from place to place or from trade to trade to make wages really competitive. Like retail prices, actual wages in each district and each trade have generally been fixed by custom—sometimes backed by combination, sometimes effective where no combination existed. And the same thing is true as to the rent of land. At the time when England and France accepted Ricardo's theories of rent without challenge, the actual rentals paid for agricultural land bore little relation to what the theory required. The landlord who raised the rent on an old tenant to a competitive level was the object of even more merciless disapproval than the shopkeeper who raised the price to an old customer.

Now the thing that distinguished the economy of the United States, and particularly of the North-western states, from that of any other country in the world is that over most of the United States for a considerable period wages and land values and even retail prices were actually fixed by free competition.

If the labourer did not like what he was getting in the factory he could move to the farm; if he did not like farm wages, it was easy to find land on which he could settle and from which he could get a living on his own account. The productivity of unoccupied land fixed a basis for wages and wage rates. Labour in the Northwestern states, and to some degree in the Northeastern, had that mobility which it lacked in Europe. The power to go somewhere else on short notice was a more effective protection to the American labouring man than strikes or unions possibly could be. In fact, labour unions hardly had a chance to exist in the country west of the Alleghanies prior to 1860, because nearly every labouring man in the whole region who had any qualities of leadership aspired to become a capitalist. And even in the East, where there was a large factory population, and where there were a good many labour disturbances in the years from 1830 to 1840, they appear to have been chiefly the work of foreign elements in the population, newly arrived and not yet assimilated.

Land values were determined in the same fashion. There was no such system of land *rents* in the United States as there has been in England because American farms were generally cultivated by their owners. Even if the cultivator had very little capital, he generally took title, paid a small portion of the price, and borrowed the rest on mortgage from the sellers. As the ownership of land conferred no social distinction, a man who had land which he did not intend to cultivate, preferred to sell it on these terms rather than lease it; he was rather better protected by a mortgage than by a lease and was free of all disputes regarding future improvements. Now when land is bought and sold after this fashion there is no room for the operation of the customs and settlements which regulate its rent in England or its price in France. The occupancy goes to the highest bidder, at full market value.

For these economic reasons, as well as for the political reasons which I have mentioned earlier, the American commonwealths of the Northwest represented the normal working out of the theories which possessed men's minds in the latter part of the eighteenth century and in most of the nineteenth. Politically they carried out the ideas of Rousseau; economically they approximated the conditions on which Adam Smith and his successors based their system. They represented the high water mark of the movement in favour of individual liberty, which was a natural reaction against the abuse of authority in Europe during the sixteenth and seventeenth centuries in matters of religion, of politics, or of trade. They represented a disbelief in sovereigns and a belief in men.

With the American people as it was then constituted, these theories vindicated themselves. Dispassionate foreign observers like de Tocqueville, while recognizing the imperfection of American society in the second quarter of the nineteenth century, were unqualified in their approval of its essential soundness and of its promise for the future; and this opinion was shared by most Americans, among the thinking class as well as the unthinking.

Nor was this to be wondered at. America's system of politics and morals had in a little over half a century enabled a weak and unorganized people of 4,000,000 to increase to a strong and adequately governed nation of 20,000,000. Her citizens were generally intelligent, prosperous, and law abiding. Her industrial methods were in the highest degree progressive. She had taken the lead in the development of the railroad, the telegraph, and modern methods of commerce. She furnished an instance where the theories of liberty in politics and in economics appeared to be justified by the results. The United States had not only secured a wide diffusion of property among her citizens, but a still wider diffusion of those *ideas* regarding property which made the institution a source of political strength. The ambition to acquire wealth acted as a universal stimulus to work, a powerful incentive to save, and an encouragement to the invention of improved machinery and more economical methods. Free competition, with as little restraint from legislative or police power as possible, had put leadership of industry into hands which were recognized as capable, and had resulted in scales of prices and rates of wages which were generally satisfactory to the public. American institutions, had, in a word, provided the necessary political and economic security with the minimum of government interference.

In all that I have been describing, the American Northwest was simply carrying out with a free hand theories of political philosophy and political economy which the thinking men of England and France accepted and tried to carry out as far as they could—principles which in one field, that of international trade, Cobden and Chevalier developed more fully than any American statesman was able to do. So far as national psychology is concerned, the history of England and France runs in many ways parallel to that of America. The constitutional development of the three countries had been very different. America built up her commonwealth by theoretical rules out of such materials as she could find; England evolved hers by first making the King's ministers responsible to Parliament and then converting her Parliament into a representative body; France reached hers through a series of revolutions which gave the people equality of civil rights at a very early period and left political equality to follow by a somewhat tortuous course. Yet in spite of all these differences the attitude of the English mind and the French mind and the

American mind towards many industrial problems
of government has undergone the same series of
changes at pretty nearly the same time.

One set of assumptions regarding human freedom
and human rights underlay the popular thinking of
all these countries in 1850; one set of phrases appealed to the popular imagination in all of them. In
1920 another set of assumptions has taken their
place; the old phrases have lost their appeal and their
potency. Liberty is no longer a name to conjure
with; democracy has taken its place. The world has
ceased to idealize the individual; it idealizes the
demos or collective body of the people instead. It no
longer cherishes the illusion that men when given
liberty will try to do right of their own accord, or
that the unfettered pursuit by each man of his own
interest will result in the common good of all. But
it has come under the equally unwarranted and still
more dangerous illusion that the people as a whole
is better and wiser than the individuals of which
it is composed; and it believes that the will of a
majority, backed by force, is likely to result in something fairer and more permanent than can come from
the trying out of separate experiments, and the inter-
play of separate ideas, which characterized the older
systems. The pathetic reliance of the Russian upon
his Soviet and everything that bears its name is but
an extreme instance of a feeling that pervades the

nations of Europe and America today. In the year 1917 a clergyman of my acquaintance came near losing his position in a parish of much more than ordinary intelligence because he said that it was no more important or difficult to make the world safe for democracy than to make democracy safe for the world.

The democratic statesman of today has a double problem. He must adapt economic institutions like property right and corporate capital, and political institutions like representative government, which were developed under the conditions and ideas of the nineteenth century, to the altered circumstances of the twentieth. He must also educate the people fast enough to enable them to pass over to the new conditions and the new institutions without sacrificing the standard of economic efficiency which they have reached under the old. If he can succeed, we may look forward to an orderly development like that of England in the last hundred and thirty years; if he fails, the best for which we can hope is a series of revolutions and reactions, like that which has befallen the continent in the same period. And his most promising chance of success lies in recognizing the fact that the individual problems of trade regulation and wage regulation, of civil liberty and of constitutional government are best understood when studied as problems in national psychology quite as much as in public law or political economy.

INDUSTRIAL COMBINATION

THE writings of John Stuart Mill give an excellent idea of the theory of national prosperity which was held by nine-tenths of the thinking men in the middle of the nineteenth century. Free competition, representative government, international comity: these formed the trinity of aspects in which the goddess of liberty revealed herself to mankind. Free competition would furnish motive for labour and thrift, opportunity for industrial progress, and reasonable assurance that the rewards for labour, thrift, and progress would be apportioned with justice among different individuals or sections of the community. Representative government would enable the members of the body politic to see that such competition was carried on fairly under laws which accorded with the public opinion of the community as a whole; and it would keep the administrative officers of the state in their true place as agents of the people, appointed to secure public safety and fair dealing at the minimum cost in the way of taxes. International comity would lead each people to understand what its neighbours could do best, and would pave the way for a division of labour between nations which would contribute as much to the industrial prosperity and peace of the civilized world as the division of labour between individuals had contributed to the prosperity and peace of the several commonwealths of which it was composed.

To the men of 1850 who either had property or expected to get some, this social philosophy seemed delightfully complete and comfortable. When Bastiat gave his book on political economy the title *Economic Harmonics*, few were found to dispute the implied claim as an unwarranted one. So great was the confidence that we had discovered the road toward the solution of all social problems that Mill himself, modest and judicial though he was, said quite boldly that economics was in many respects a finished science, and that nothing in the fundamental laws of value remained to be cleared up. Europe in the middle of the last century was profoundly and confidently individualistic. It believed that in economics, in politics and in morals, the man who pursued his own interest intelligently worked for the best interests of society as a whole.

The protests which had been registered against this view had tended to confirm it rather than to weaken it. Socialistic philosophies had been discredited by the results of their own experiments whenever they had had a chance to put their views into practice. When the Young-Hegelians, headed by Karl Marx, confined their theories to paper, they sounded plausible enough; but when the revolution of 1848 gave them the opportunity to use public credit for the establishment of national workshops the failure was as complete and the disproof as convincing as the most ardent individualist could have desired. Voices there were—like those of Carlyle or Kingsley or Ruskin—which complained of the unfairness of free competition and the futility of representative government; but they were voices of men crying in the wilderness, supported only by a somewhat inarticulate mass of the discontented, and nearly drowned out by the jubilant chorus of optimists by which they were surrounded.

But what do we find today after the lapse of seventy years? The complacent optimism of Mill and the business men of Mill's day changed to a state of anxious unrest; Carlyle and Ruskin no longer regarded as spokesmen of a negligible minority but as prophets of coming majorities; liberty treated as a doubtful good, to be cast aside, if necessary, in the pursuit of the *ignis fatuus* of equality. If this last seems a strong expression, we have only to look at the present state of Russia, where millions of people have been content to submit passively to an arbitrary group of rulers and endure the utmost misery under their rule, in order to be sure that others are no better off than they.

The change, as I regard it, is the result of three

separate movements of thought; an economic movement resulting from the partial failure of free competition to accomplish what was expected of it; a political
movement, resulting from a change in the character
of representative government under modern industrial
conditions; and a psychological movement resulting
from—or perhaps we should rather say resulting *in*—
the substitution of international jealousy for international comity as a determining force in foreign
politics. Although these movements are hard to dis-
entangle from one another, I think we shall gain in
clearness of thinking if we try to analyse them
separately. I shall therefore make each of them the
subject of a distinct lecture; drawing my main illustra-
tions from American history, but trying to explain
at the same time some of the more significant differences between America and Europe. In this lecture
I shall deal with the economic movement resulting
from the partial failure of free competition.

At the risk of repeating what most of us already
know, I am going to begin by stating what the theory
of free competition really was; for it has suffered
much from the distortions of its enemies, and scarcely
less from the well-meant elucidations of its friends.

In an old-fashioned public market, where the producers offer their wares for sale, and the consumers
or their representatives come to buy them, prices
might be determined in any one of three ways; by

custom, by bargaining, or by competition. Each of
the first two methods had serious disadvantages.
A price fixed by custom might be so high as to
frighten away buyers, so that many people who had
brought goods to market would have to take them
home again unsold; or, still more commonly, it might
be so low that the whole supply of the article in the
market would be exhausted at an early hour and many
purchasers be unable to get what they wanted at any
cost. A price fixed by bargaining varied according
to the personal characteristics of the buyer and seller,
and usually varied in the wrong direction; the gain
accruing to the unscrupulous, the loss to the self-
respecting. It was found better to rely on competition; to let the seller make what price he pleased, but
encourage the buyer to go at once to somebody else
if the price was too high, instead of stopping to
bargain. Under this system, the man who had a
comparatively low fixed price, and stuck to it squarely,
sold his goods; while the man who tried to browbeat
his customers at the beginning was forced to make
concessions at the end. If sellers could appeal to
different buyers and buyers resort to different sellers,
the result was a competitive price which *cleared the
market*—a fair market price in the old English sense.
And this system had the additional advantage that
if the market price of an article was unduly high, on
account of scarcity, the profit which it offered was

the surest way to attract more sellers to that market in the next quarter. To limit the price was to perpetuate the scarcity; to leave it free was to allow temporary profit to a few producers, but to get permanent advantage for the consumers.

Now the political economy of Smith or Ricardo or Mill was simply an attempt to apply this system to *all* transactions of our industrial world; to let the man who had capital to invest go into the labour market today and buy his labour at what price he could; trusting that the goods produced by this labour, when sold by him in the nearest wholesale market, would remunerate him for the expenses incurred and leave him a reasonable margin of profit. As long as there was capital seeking investment, this fact would compel the individual capitalist to pay the labourer a fair market rate, and would prevent him from charging the consumer such prices as would allow him an extraordinary rate of profit for any length of time. Thus the self-interest of capitalists competing with one another would make fair rates of wages that would clear the labour market, fair rates of interest that would clear the money market, and fair scales of prices that would clear the wholesale and retail markets. Any attempt by law or by combination to obtain higher wages, lower rates of interest, or lower prices, than the competitive sale provided, would defeat its own purpose by checking the accumulation of capital, the demand for labour, and the supply of consumable goods.

The ideals of economic freedom accorded so well with the prevalent views regarding political liberty, that statesmen were quite content to accept them as reasoned truths, without enquiring too closely whether the conception of the industrial world as a large public market corresponded to the real facts in the case. But the actual correspondence was not nearly so close as our fathers thought. The position of the large factory owners who are buying labour differs from that of the customers in a public market who are buying the products of labour. The position of the railway companies which are selling transportation differs still more radically from that of stall-keepers in a public market who are selling goods. Nominally there is free competition among factory owners or railway owners; actually the workman finds it hard to deal with more than one factory, and the shipper finds it yet harder to deal with more than one railway. It makes no difference to the situation that the factory has no legal monopoly. Modern industrial improvements have given the large establishment such an advantage over the small one in the matter of operating costs that monopoly may exist *de facto* even if discountenanced *de jure*, and consolidation take place whether we like it or not.

Each of these facts when recognized gives a

democratic state a new and somewhat unwelcome problem to deal with. Things which we had expected to leave to individuals, in full confidence that they would work out rightly under a system of liberty, now become the subject of organized action. To a monarchic state the situation presents no such serious problem. Monarchies are arranged for organized collective action as a fundamental theory, and collective bargaining fits into their system easily enough. If liberty works wrong your monarchist simply says "I told you so." He has no railway problem, in the English or American sense, because he stands for state railways on principle. He has no widespread interruptions of public service through strikes, because he is prepared to imprison without delay the men who are responsible for such interruptions. For the sake of avoiding these difficulties which have beset England and America the old-school Prussian was content to accept the dangers—to my mind the far greater dangers—that menace the nation in which discipline has been made to take the place of self-control.

But for the Englishman or American the problem is more complex. He is not content to leave matters to a government commission; partly because he is less confident than the Prussian that the decisions of such a body will be wholly wise or disinterested, and partly because he fears that the suppression (actual or

threatened) of individual liberty in the industrial field
will destroy the initiative and self-reliance of the
people in other fields and ultimately menace freedom
itself. Democracy thus has a harder problem than
monarchy. It must deal with railway organizations
or with labour organizations in such a way as to leave
as much as possible of the initiative and the responsibility in their hands; but it must at the same time be
always watchful to prevent the power thus given from
becoming a public menace.

Of the problems which arise when a single large
corporation is selling goods or services to a number
of different buyers, the railway has furnished the
earliest and clearest example. Its history need not
delay us very long; for the general course of railway
legislation in England and in America has been so
nearly the same that little explanation is required
beyond a bare recital of events. First there was a
period which lasted till about 1845 in England and
till about 1870 in America when people tried to shut
their eyes to the fact that there *was* any problem;
saying that railroads could be made to compete by the
building of parallel lines or by allowing independent
carriers to run trains on the same lines. When it
finally appeared that parallel lines were wasteful and
that competition of different carriers on the same line
was impossible, each country passed to the second
period of regulation, which lasted pretty nearly

through the nineteenth century. In this period most people still held that competition might in the long run be trusted to regulate railway profits, and the general scale of railway charges; but they saw the evils which resulted from the arbitrary power of the railway manager to give *preferences* to one locality or one individual to the detriment of another. It was against such preferences and discriminations that the British Railway Acts of 1854 and 1873, and the American Interstate Commerce Act of 1887 were chiefly directed.

Much good came of all these acts; more perhaps than people at the present day are ready to recognize. But in the closing years of the last century shippers in both our countries came to feel that we had dealt with only a part of the problem and perhaps not the most important part. Competition did not always prevent railroad rates from being kept unduly high; and high rates were almost as intolerable to the community as unequal rates. Two causes combined to produce this state of public feeling. The well-established main lines in each country—"trunk lines" we call them in America—by their superior location and by their monopoly of the best terminal facilities were put in position to receive a permanent profit or economic rent from this source. Now economic rent has always formed an object of jealousy, and large owners who exact all the rent they can get are very unpopular; nor did the railways escape this unpopularity. It was heightened in America by the fact that our railways were generally owned in the East while a large proportion of the freight shipments originated in the West, so that we suffered, and still suffer, from the evils of absentee ownership. But of yet more influence than this jealousy of rent, was a growing perception of the fact that the special problems of railways or gas works or other forms of public service corporations were but incidents in a general problem; that the tendency of every industry with large fixed capital was to combine into an association of some form—call it what you will, "pool" or "conference," "trust" or "consolidation"; that any such association was in large degree independent of the old checks of free competition; and that many of the consolidations which took place in America at the close of the last century had been made an excuse for the issue of "watered stock"—of shares which represented no actual investment, but a capitalized expectation of future profit. Inasmuch as the issue of railway shares in America had never been adequately regulated by the states, there was a good deal of such water in some of our railroad capital; and the public was quite ready to believe that amount to be much greater than it really was.

Under these circumstances commissions and courts, which had hitherto been charged with the comparatively simple problem of securing relative equality in railway rates, were brought face to face with the far more difficult problem of finding absolute standards on which to base their schedules—weighing the conflicting claims of railway capital, railway labour, and the public which the railways serve. Our success in dealing with this problem in America has not yet been very great. The authorities have worked hard and tried to do justice to all parties; but both courts and commissions have tended to lose sight of the fact that in order to give the community the advantage of low rates we must stimulate labour and capital to the utmost efficiency. While the great majority of American rate decisions can be defended on plausible grounds, the general effect of such decisions has been to prevent enough new money and enough new brains from going into railroad service to keep up the standards of progress or efficiency set by the last century. And when progress and efficiency stop, costs go up and the public suffers—commission or no commission. I shall not attempt to decide how far recent English experience accords with that of America: but west of the Atlantic the principle of collective bargaining under the advice of public authorities has failed, for the simple and all-sufficient reason that we have not recognized the primary necessity of putting efficiency into the foreground.

And it is this same lack of necessary intelligence

for collective bargaining, and this readiness to over-look the primary importance of industrial efficiency to a democracy, which constitute the cardinal diffi-culties in dealing with the American labour problem. For this part of our task we seem worse equipped than England.

The general history of the labour problem, as handled by the Anglo-Saxon on the two sides of the Atlantic, has been alike in its essential features. The English or American labourer has relied more on organized effort within the framework of the existing social system than on discussion of means to over-throw that system. He has put more trust in the chief of his union than in the revolutionary agitator. His primary object has been to form combinations of wage workers strong enough to deal with the large units of organized capital which the modern factory system has developed. Where there was a chance that legislation would help him in regulating the condi-tions of factory employment or the terms and impli-cations of the wage contract, he has taken occasion to avail himself of such help; but in the main issue, as to what price he should be paid for his services, he has until recently relied much more upon what he and his associates could do for themselves than upon what government could do for them. The part of this story which concerns England has been so fully and on the whole so fairly told by Mr and Mrs Webb that I do not need to go into it in detail. I am sure it will meet the wishes of an English audience better, and serve the purpose of this lectureship more fully, if I centre my attention on the *differences* in the history of the labour movement on the two sides of the Atlantic and explain them as well as I can.

The labour union did not develop in America nearly as soon as it did in England. We hear something of it in 1817 and 1818, and much more in the years from 1833 to 1837; but the national questions of public policy which it involved were hardly recognized until the decade from 1870 to 1880. The reasons for this are not far to seek. The factory system of America came much later into being than that of England. When it first developed there was no social gulf between mill-owners and mill-hands. In the South, where such a gulf would undoubtedly have existed, there were hardly any factories. In the North and still more conspicuously in the West there were no well-defined social lines. Even where the owners were a good deal richer than the operatives, the living conditions of owner and operative were not so widely apart. Their children went to the same schools and had much the same interests. There was scarcely an enterprising man among the operatives who did not cherish the ambition to become a capitalist before he died. And, last but not least, the wages themselves when measured in purchasing power were very high. So long as there was free land, an able-bodied man could get a good living for himself and his family by cultivating it; and if the factory wanted to keep him the factory had to compete with the farm for his services. Not that America was a labourer's paradise. Hours were always long, working conditions often unsanitary. But there was nothing to encourage the organization or even the prejudice of labourers as a class against capitalists as a class. And except in those towns which had a large foreign population this general state of things continued till after the Civil War.

But in the years from 1865 to 1873 there was a large influx of foreign immigrants of a kind very different from that which came over in the earlier years of the republic. Instead of the self-reliant man who was fitted by temperament to adapt himself to American conditions, we now had an increasing proportion of "assisted" immigrants—some brought over by American capitalists, under contract to pay their passage by working for them after their arrival, some lured by the glowing promises of the steamship company's agents—and not a few who under the persuasion of home or family authorities "had left their country for their country's good." In the years of prosperity and thoughtlessness which preceded the crisis of 1873 the dangers arising from the pressure of this element were overlooked; but when the panic came and wages fell America found herself face to face with a different kind of labour situation from any that had been possible in any earlier commercial crisis.

It was most unfortunate for the history of trade unionism in the United States that its first real test had been deferred until this time and came under just these conditions. For it had the effect of putting the unions into the apparent position of enemies to public security and prosperity; and the impression made at that time has never been wholly outgrown.

A strike may be regarded in two ways; as a contest between employer and employee to see which can bring the other to terms, or as an enforced stoppage of production throughout the community which will cause hardship and loss to consumers who are in no wise responsible for the management of the industry involved. If the strike affects only a portion of the available supply, it may be regarded in the former aspect, as a contest between employee and employer, which they can be left to fight out as best they may. But if it takes away the whole supply of services or goods available in any locality, as in a railway strike or a widespread coal miners' strike, it at once becomes a matter of grave public concern; and any party to such a dispute which ignores the public interest and affects to treat the matter as a private one, deserves and incurs public condemnation, independent of the merits of the immediate issue involved.

The English labour unions had had the advantage of making their first experiments before the full development of the modern railway system or the modern public service corporation. They tried out their powers in manufacturing strikes, where the direct hardship to the outside public from the closing of a factory or group of factories was not very great. The leaders learned lessons in self-control and conservatism at the expense of the parties directly involved, without creating unnecessary antagonism in the general public. What might have happened in case they had made their early experiments with public service corporations is illustrated by what occurred in 1837, when an ill-advised strike of gas stokers in Westminster, which deprived citizens of light for some weeks, produced a widespread reaction against the whole trade union movement in Parliament, in the courts, and in public sentiment, whose effect lasted for many years.

Now what might have happened in England was what actually did happen in America. The first great object lesson which was given the American public as to the possibilities of trades-unionism came in October, 1876, on the New Jersey Central Railroad between New York and Philadelphia. The time was one of great depression in railroad business, and there had been reductions of working force and of wages; but the immediate question raised by this strike and others that followed it, was not one of working force or wages, but one of control. The railway corporation had a duty to perform continuous public service; the Brotherhood of Locomotive Engineers had it in its power to make continuous service impossible, except on terms which it approved; the more completely the existence of this power was demonstrated to the public the more fully the rights of the Brotherhood could be recognized—at least so they expected.

"The characteristics of these strikes," says Mr Charles Francis Adams in his official report, "were unmistakable. There was a perfect organization; and once they were decided upon they were carried out with promptness and decision, regardless of public inconvenience or private loss." The strike on the Central of New Jersey, the first of this series, was inaugurated by a note making complaint of the engineers' grievances on the line and requesting the corporation to confer at once with the Chief of the Brotherhood concerning their removal. "As this did not lead to the desired result a strike was authorized at once, and the corporation was notified that, unless the concessions asked for were made, the men would leave their engines at twelve o'clock that very night. A request for further time was rejected, and at midnight of October 23–4 every train on the road was hauled to the nearest siding and the locomotives abandoned,

their fires being first drawn. On the morning of the
24th, not a wheel was in motion on the entire road.
As the Central of New Jersey, in addition to being
a heavy carrier of coal, is one of the great suburban
lines running out from New York City, the immense
public and private inconvenience occasioned by this
sudden stoppage of all movement over it can be
imagined. In addition to this, however, the strike
took place in the midst of the heavy Centennial Ex-
position travel of that season; and great hardship was
suffered by those who chanced to be in the abandoned
trains. Under these circumstances the officials deemed
it inexpedient to attempt any further resistance, and
accordingly all the demands of the engineers were
acceded to. The men then returned to work, and, after
a suspension of twenty-four hours, traffic was resumed
on the morning of the 25th."

Three weeks later a similar strike took place on
the Cairo and St Louis road, a thousand miles distant,
and was accompanied by rioting and violence. Here,
however, the strikers were defeated. Hardly had the
public received news of the St Louis strike when a
third strike broke out in Georgia, with indecisive
results. Six weeks later, on December 29, 1876, a
still more remarkable strike took place on the Grand
Trunk Railway of Canada. "The difficulty originated
in the discharge by the company of certain of its
engineers, members of the Brotherhood. Notice of

an intention to strike at 9 p.m. of that day, unless
the required concessions were previously made, was
given to the officials at 7 p.m. of December 29; and
at the hour named every train in motion on that
portion of the line west of Montreal was stopped and
the locomotive fires drawn. This made a complete
block, as the road had but a single track; and the
difficulty of the situation, so far as the company was
concerned, was further aggravated by a heavy snow-
storm. The next day an attempt was made to get the
trains in motion in charge of new men; but these
were assaulted and driven away, while the engines
were run off the track and snow ploughs put across
it. The round-houses also were in the hands of the
mob. This condition of affairs lasted until the 3rd of
January, when the company gave way, yielding all
the points at issue."

Apparently the Brotherhood had won a complete
victory at small cost. Actually the victory was short-
lived, the cost immeasurable. For the effect of these
acts was to convert friends of the Brotherhood into
neutrals and neutrals into enemies; and to arouse
among the more ignorant American labourers aim-
less outbreaks of lawlessness which the Brotherhood
leaders neither foresaw nor countenanced. The public
reaction undid all and more than all that the success
of a few strikes had accomplished, and left the
companies in a stronger position at the end of 1877,

and the unions in a weaker one, than they had held a year earlier.

The Brotherhood chiefs learned their lesson; and for nearly forty years afterwards that organization was a conservative force in the labour situation of the country. But the public had also learned a lesson— or thought it had. It was confirmed in its belief in the fundamental rightness of the open shop principle. It apprehended public danger from any plan which demanded that all the employees in a given industry should be members of a union; and this apprehension was confirmed when other organizations, less experienced than the Locomotive Engineers, continued until the end of the century to repeat the same kind of experiments. Such was the story of the coal strikes of 1878 and 1879, of the telegraphers' strike of 1883, of the series of strikes organized by the "Knights of Labour" from 1885 to 1888, and of the Pullman strike of 1894. Whatever the actual merits of the several contests, the strikers managed to put themselves in the wrong by their manner of conducting them.

It was not I think until the beginning of the present century that a prolonged contest was conducted by American labour leaders with any thoroughly intelligent understanding or regard for what the outside public really thought. The great anthracite coal strike of 1902 gave the first indication that labour unions were learning to assume that responsibility to public opinion which public service corporations had already been compelled to accept. The demands of the labour leaders, whether justified or not, were at any rate clearly stated; and they were presented long enough in advance to give opportunity for full discussion. Instead of beginning the strike at the opening of winter, in order to produce the maximum effect of shortage, the unions deferred it till spring. And, though they were not very scrupulous about breaking agreements within the trade or encouraging sympathetic strikes where no real grievance existed, they showed praiseworthy self-control in abstaining from acts of violence.

On the part of the capitalists, this strike was not wisely handled. They talked too much and did too little. They did not use the half dozen summer months to protect the public against scarcity of coal, either by encouraging importation or by making the public familiar with the real state of affairs. They were content to predict that the strike would be over in a few weeks. But months passed and winter came, and the strike was not over. Under these circumstances public sentiment was, on the whole, with the strikers. When the advent of freezing weather caused actual suffering, the pressure upon the companies for the immediate settlement of the dispute was so strong that President Roosevelt took it upon himself to interfere; and production was resumed under conditions which, while they fell short of an absolute victory for the strikers, yet gave them a large part of the things for which they had contended.

The success of the United Mine Workers in the contest did not lead the American Federation of Labour to precipitate action. Men like Mitchell or Gompers knew that the position of the unions in America was much weaker than in England. To begin with, a majority of the productive labourers of the United States were unorganized, and likely to remain so for some time. In spite of all the changes that had taken place since the Civil War, small farmers were quite as numerous as factory hands or mine workers. In the next place, the number of competent trade-union leaders who knew just how much to claim in negotiations with capitalists, or what points to put forward in appeals to the public, was relatively small—much smaller than in England— and their control over their followers less secure. The emotional element still predominated very largely over the intellectual in American labour organizations and in the discussions by which they were swayed. Finally, outside public sentiment was still flatly for the open shop principle, and against every attempt to deprive a man of the chance to work unless he was a member of some particular organization; and President Roosevelt fully shared the public view in this respect. Under these circumstances the labour leaders acted wisely in biding their time until public sentiment should become more favourable, and a man of somewhat different temper should sit in the President's chair. For thirteen years they gradually strengthened their position, abstaining from spectacular strikes during two periods of industrial depression, until they saw their opportunity for bringing the labour question into politics under favourable conditions, in the summer of 1916.

The year 1915 had been a period of large demand for the products of American labour and decided advances in wages. There had been no corresponding advances in railroad rates; and under these circumstances the managers did not feel able to increase the wages of engineers or trainmen. In the spring of 1916 the unions presented a demand for such an increase, to correspond to the rates which were paid for similar services in other industries. They gave full time for consideration of this proposal, but threatened a general strike if it was not complied with. I myself felt at the time that this demand should have been granted; and that the claim of the railroad employees to the same wages which prevailed in other industries would then become a most effective help in securing the needed increase in railroad rates. But a majority of railroad managers thought otherwise. They were doubtful whether the needed rate increase would follow the wage increase. They believed that they were then strong enough to run the roads in despite of the unions, while if they yielded at that time they might not be strong enough next time.

The result was disastrous to the companies. Faced with the proposal of stoppage of traffic, both President Wilson and the majority of Congress took the side of the labourers, and passed an Act known as the Adamson Law, requiring the management to accede to the demands of the unions. Having the confidence of the President and the support of the majority in Congress the labour leaders were able to increase their advantage during the period of government operation which followed America's entrance into the world war; carrying the "standardization" of wages to an extreme, and introducing the principle that railway managers should deal with representatives of national labour unions, instead of with committees of their own men, in all disputed matters affecting labour. In many of these respects the railway managers have not been able to return to the old system since the resumption of operation by the companies in 1919.

But outside of railway service, the general position of trade unions has not become stronger as a result of the war. In spite of the growth of manufacturing and the increase of foreign born population, the bulk of the American people is still for the open shop. This was shown conclusively by the elections in 1919 and 1920, where candidates who had openly defied the labour leaders received unexpectedly large majorities and where President Wilson himself lost far more than he gained by being regarded as a supporter of the union claims.

The American public fears trade-union influence on two grounds; first, because it believes that union leaders are attempting to create privileged classes or groups of labourers who will be able to command higher wages than other labourers in the same community get for similar services; and second, because it fears that the unions stand for less efficient methods of work than prevailed under the competitive system. In each of these respects the policy of the railway unions during the war and the years that followed the war has tended to confirm the public apprehension rather than to remove it.

For while America sees that free competition has failed to secure *all* the good which we expected from it, she also sees that it has accomplished two or three great things. It has come nearer than any other system ever has to rewarding men for the service they did rather than for the number of days they spent in doing it; and it has thereby promoted a degree of industrial efficiency, individual and collective, which has been of the highest service to the nation at home and abroad. Any system of standardization which makes equal pay for work of different quality, or prevents promotion and advance by merit, seems like a step backward, which has more of danger in it than of promise. Any set of regulations which attempts to increase the wages of a class or group of labourers by lessening the public service which they are allowed or encouraged to do, not only seems but is a step toward the creation of a privileged class, and a menace to the business and the public spirit of the community. There may be times when it is desirable to limit the output of certain lines of goods, with a view of making production more regular, and fluctuations in price or in employment less severe; but the attempt to lessen the services which labourers of any given class can render the public, whether by direct limitation of production or by the retention of inefficient methods, is an attack on the strength of the nation as a whole. A dispute about the terms of the labour contract under modern conditions is not a matter which chiefly concerns the immediate parties interested; it is one which concerns the public as a whole, and is to be settled from that standpoint. A generation ago the large capitalists tried to ignore this fact, and were defeated in their attempt. Today, the American labour leaders, with a few honourable exceptions, are still prone to ignore it. As long as this continues the American public will be for the "open shop."

Of the political elements in the American labour problem, as distinct from the industrial elements, I shall speak in the next lecture.

COLLECTIVE BARGAINING IN POLITICS

WE have seen in the two previous lectures how free competition was tried in America under exceptionally favourable conditions; and, for a time, with remarkably good results in national character and national efficiency. We have also seen how, in spite of these conditions and results, competition failed to maintain itself unimpaired in the face of the growing tendency toward industrial combination, which is manifest all over the world. In this lecture I shall try to show how industrial combination has been attended by political combination in America and in other countries with representative government; how collective organization of industry has been a powerful stimulus to collective bargaining in politics; how the so-called "block" system is tending to displace, and in some instances has already displaced, the party system in legislative assemblies. Industrial combination has given the statesman of the twentieth century a new set of problems with which to deal; political combination has weakened the efficiency of old methods and old institutions for dealing with these problems.

Let us begin the discussion of this aspect of the

subject by a statement of the old theory of parliamentary government.

In the ancient city-states like those of Greece, the democratic element in the commonwealth was represented by the *ecclesia* or general assembly of citizens— the town meeting as we still call it in New England— which discussed the conduct of magistrates, voted on questions of foreign policy and regulated the levying and expenditure of money. The town meetings were not legislative assemblies in the modern sense. Any law making they did was purely incidental. They were agencies for keeping the administration and public opinion in accord; and as long as a city remained small they served this purpose tolerably well. But when the city grew large ancient democracies were helpless. Real discussion by the whole body of freemen proved to be an impossibility. Assemblies became places of disorder, rather than means of good government; and no machinery was at hand to take their place.

Modern democracies were more fortunate. They found in the English Parliament of the eighteenth century an institution which, though originally devised for the benefit of the privileged classes, had done much to give shape and power to the public opinion of the whole nation, and might with some changes be made to do this more completely.

The military and social conditions of the thirteenth

and fourteenth centuries were such that monarchs who wished to consolidate and build up their power over any great area like that of England or France or Spain often had to secure the co-operation of the nobility, the church, and the property owners—not only the landholders of the country but the guilds of the city. If they attempted to levy new taxes without first consulting these bodies or their representatives, they found it almost impossible to collect them promptly. Under these circumstances they resorted to the expedient of summoning parliaments for the discussion of the taxes proposed and of the purposes for which they were to be used. These early parliaments were not representative assemblies in the modern sense; they were hardly to be called legislative assemblies in the modern sense; but ill-defined as were their character and powers they exercised an important control over the public purse and a still more important influence in the formation of public opinion. In an age when there was no telegraph and very little postal service, when there were no newspapers or books and when few people could read or write, it was a matter of great moment to have men called together from different parts of the country and different sections of society who could tell each other what their friends were thinking and doing. Even if the nominal powers of such an assembly were small, its actual influence was large. If it included a considerable number of free and outspoken men, privileged against arrest, its power to withhold consent to taxes and to organize public opinion was often sufficient to compel the monarch to modify his policy, or at least to defer its execution, in compliance with the views of his parliament.

This kind of limitation was of course disagreeable to the monarch himself; and when kings felt strong enough they usually tried to do without parliaments, or to reduce their power to a nullity. In France and Spain they succeeded in accomplishing this; in England during the early Tudor period, it looked as if they were going to succeed. But after two centuries of struggle with varying fortune, they failed; and in the revolution of 1688, Parliament came out of the struggle a victor, assured of all its old powers of supervision and with a prospect of constant increase in authority as time went on.

Every dispassionate observer in the following century recognized that this triumph of Parliament meant a victory for good government. Bad as were the means used by Walpole or Bute to secure power and to retain it, the actual exercise of that power under Walpole and Bute was fairer and more enlightened than the exercise of power by the King's ministers in France or Spain. By contrast with its neighbours, eighteenth century England was a striking example of the good which comes from the open discussion of public questions by leading men from all parts of the country assembled under constitutional safeguards. The English Parliament showed the world a way of governing the affairs of large nations by public sentiment; a modern substitute for the *ecclesia* or town meeting, when the commonwealth became too large for any considerable proportion of its citizens to be present in person. The fact that the English House of Commons of two hundred years ago was not a representative body in any true sense of the word, made its success seem even more impressive. For if a House, composed largely of members of pocket boroughs in whose election the modern industrial England had no share, nevertheless voiced the public opinion of the community with such effect, what might not be expected when the affairs of government were in charge of a Parliament which was really representative?

So reasoned Montesquieu; so thought many of the founders of the American commonwealth in 1789. The framers of the Constitution of the United States, following the advice of French publicists, took the best model they could find—the British—and adapted it to their own peculiar conditions. Instead of a hereditary monarch they provided for an elected president; instead of one central Parliament they had state assemblies to make local laws, and a National Congress to legislate on matters when uniform and simultaneous action was necessary; instead of an unwritten constitution which changed automatically with changes in usage, they were bound by a written instrument, which the courts interpreted and enforced; one which could not be changed, except so far as judicial interpretation changed it, without formal appeal to the people of the several states. But in spite of these differences the *mechanism* of government in America under George Washington was remarkably like that of England under William Pitt. The fundamental differences lay in the fact that the American Congress in 1790 was a representative body in a way that the English Parliament was not; that its members were elected by the votes of freemen as a body while the members of the English House of Commons were then and for many years afterwards representatives of certain privileged groups— often very small ones.

Theoretically, this change looked wholly good. It gave different sections of the community equal voice in electing members of the Parliamentary assembly and equal chance to have their views urged in its debates. But practically, certain dangers developed in connection with the character and conception of Congress as a representative body, which have proved quite serious in their effect.

The fact that the American Congress was made up of representatives of a number of different districts approximately equal in population, gave many a member the idea that he was sent to Washington primarily to urge the views and enforce the claims of his district, rather than to see what was best for the public good. This had a series of evil effects. Unconsciously to himself it put the member who accepted this view on a lower plane. Instead of being a servant of the public, chosen to do what he thought best for the nation, he became an agent of a district, retained to represent the views of the majority in his district and to promote the district's interests. Of course the actual conflict between his duty to the district and his duty to the nation would not come up very frequently. If he was an honest man he would let his constituents know his ideas on public questions before they elected him; and if they voted for him after he had made such a statement, he had the right to assume that his views had their support. But suppose he changed his mind as a result of what he heard at Washington: should he vote according to his convictions or should he be bound by his actual or implied promises to those who had sent him? Or suppose that a new question came into prominence, which had not looked important at the time of his election, on which the member knew that his views differed from those of a majority of the electors in his district: should he vote according to his own conviction or according to theirs? I believe that English-

men in general would say that under either of these
circumstances a man should vote according to his
convictions, and would think that if he did not
he was sacrificing his conscience to his political
prospects. I am afraid that a great majority of
people in the United States would take a different
view, justifying the man who voted as his constituents felt, and regarding the man who was
bound by his own convictions as old-fashioned or
Quixotic.

Any such mental attitude as this, among the
members of a legislative assembly or among the outside public toward its members, greatly impairs
its usefulness as a means of forming public opinion.
When men went from all parts of the country to
debate concerning the nation's interest; to convince
others if possible, to be convinced if necessary, to
vote according to their convictions in any event; then
a parliamentary or congressional debate was a live
thing. The speech which turned the vote of a dozen
members might turn the current of public opinion
in the country, and help to build up a sentiment
throughout the nation which was more important
than any law which the representative assembly could
enact. But if men are sent to Congress or to Parliament simply to register opinions already formed in
their several districts, the speeches of the leaders will
be defensive rather than convincing, while those of

the rank and file will tend to degenerate into mere talk—"hot air" as we call it in America. They will voice the emotions of their constituents in a way that will ensure their continued popularity in their own districts rather than attempt to consolidate the sentiment of the country behind them.

In America this is what actually happens today. The public opinion of the country is formed outside of Congress, not inside its halls. The standard of congressional oratory has declined. Men who have it in their power to convince their fellows seek other means than parliamentary debate. Neither Roosevelt nor Wilson—our two twentieth century orators whose words have swayed public opinion—won his power in Congress. Our organized and effective agency for forming public opinion is the press—particularly the newspaper press. A journalist of ability wields an influence over the thoughts and feelings of his fellow-citizens to which few Congressmen can aspire. The American legislative assembly in nine cases out of ten registers the results of movements of thought which other men have shaped. And I believe that what has happened in America is rapidly taking place in other countries—that England and France and Germany look less to their Parliaments and more to their public press for guidance as to how they shall think; and that the life of a Parliamentary leader in any of these countries becomes, each decade in increasing measure, a work of reconciling and compromising opinions already formed until he can get a majority, rather than one of moulding opinion in Parliament and outside of it, into conformity with his own views.

But when Congress or Parliament ceases to be a place for developing public opinion, and acts as an agency for legislation by collective bargaining, it finds itself ill-adapted to the purpose. It becomes, almost in the nature of things, what Aristotle would call a perverted form of government; a place where certain elements or parts of the community try to shape the legislative policy of the nation for their own benefit, rather than for the benefit of the whole community. The people who adopt this policy seldom understand the wrong they are doing. They hold to the comfortable belief that if you give every district a fair and equal chance by making representation proportionate to population, the resulting laws are bound to be fair to all in the long run. Of course this belief has little foundation in fact; and if it had ten times more than it has, it would not prove that equality of treatment for all the parts meant that the whole body politic was progressing in the right direction. It is simply one of those political superstitions which make people think they are doing right when they are really doing wrong, and exemplify so clearly the point made by the French essayist that "virtue is more dangerous than vice because its excesses are not subject to the restraints of conscience."

To take one instance among many—the American tariff for more than half a century has been the result of compromises between different districts, rather than of general agreement upon principles. As we look back on the successive tariff acts we can see that large sections of them were not beneficial to the nation as a whole; that in the effort to secure support in this or that locality Congress purchased relatively small advantages at large cost, and imposed duties which no economist, whether free trader or protectionist, would now attempt to defend. Another instance, almost equally striking, is being furnished in connection with the budgets of the country in recent years. A large part of our federal taxation is paid by four or five states out of a total of ten times that number. Under these circumstances there is a constant tendency to undertake works of reclamation, or road building, or public education, where the expenditure will be pretty equally divided among the many states represented in Congress while the resulting burden is largely carried by the few. The economic evils to the whole nation, direct and indirect, which may result from such legislation in the avowed interest of the majority, and from the state of mind which makes this legislation possible, are so obvious that I need hardly dwell upon them.

It may be laid down as a general principle that whoever tries to make laws for a whole nation to obey, be he member of Congress or of Parliament, judge of a court or president of a commission of experts, must regard himself as bound by a single duty to the people as a whole and not by a paramount obligation to any part of it. So far as our present methods of legislation by representative assembly involve a violation of this principle, they are bad methods and will tend to produce bad laws.

They will also tend to interfere with the proper performance of the main work of government—the protection of the liberties of the individual and the administration of the collective business of the community.

In modern democracies we are sometimes tempted to lose sight of the fact that this *is* the main work of government. We have interested ourselves so much in Congresses and Parliaments that we think of parliamentary debate and of legislation by representative assembly as bulwarks of freedom and almost as ends in themselves. Now whatever they are, they are not ends in themselves. Debate in representative assemblies is valuable as a means of forming public opinion, in the assembly and out of it. If it is used for other and antagonistic purposes the less we have of it the better. Legislation by representative assembly is valuable as a means of giving effect to public opinion. If it goes beyond public opinion or is urged as a substitute for public opinion by reformers whose zeal exceeds their discretion the less we have of it the better. The debate and the legislation resulting from debate are both a mere incident in the work of good government, and not the main work. That is done by the administration—in a democracy no less than in a monarchy. We could not get along for a single day without the police and the officers of the courts; we should find it hard to live a week without the action of the health service, and the lighthouse service, and the postal service—not to speak of the various financial agencies of the government. But we can and do get on without legislative assemblies for many months at a time, and no one misses them. In fact the tendency in most of the states of the American union in recent years has been to get along without them as much as we could; either by refusing to let our state legislatures meet oftener than once in two years, or by limiting their powers to pass laws of importance without referring them to the people.

But whether legislation be good or bad, and whether legislative assemblies meet often or seldom, one thing is clear; their presence must not be allowed to prevent the administration of the country from being carried on continuously, efficiently, and economically. A house divided against itself cannot stand. If democracy results in conflicts between different branches of the government in such a way as to prevent good administration, democracy is doomed to give way to some better system.

The traditional way of avoiding such conflicts was devised in England. During the seventeenth and eighteenth centuries a system of parties and of party machinery was developed which was generally sufficient to enable the ministers and the parliamentary majority to work together as one government instead of two.

In every strong and progressive modern state the citizens have generally tended to divide themselves into two groups on broad questions of constitutional theory. Just what form the line of cleavage has taken has depended on the special circumstances of each particular country. In England or France the permanent issue which overshadowed all temporary ones in importance was the same as it had been in commonwealths of the ancient world—a division between conservatives who regarded class privileges and vested rights as essential to public welfare, and liberals who regarded them (or many of them) as obstructions to freedom and progress. In America, Switzerland or Germany the practical question was a different one, and the line of cleavage differed correspondingly. The practical question was not how to limit the power of a sovereign or of a privileged class without destroying all existing authority, but how to create a strong central government without upsetting local government. Under these circumstances people divided into federalists who wanted to give a larger sphere of influence to the governmental organs of the federations, and states-rights men who were more concerned to preserve the liberties of the several parts. But in all these cases the issue on constitutional theory was so continuous and so important that members of either party could be trusted to work with the party and to vote with the party leaders whenever a vote on the other side would have the effect of putting the opposite party in power.

When the members of assemblies thus divide on questions of public policy—when in other words there are two well-defined parties with only a small floating vote that is unattached to either group—parliamentary government, as we have known it in the past, is relatively easy to maintain. The administration can judge how far and how long the legislature will give the necessary support to its measures. So long as it has a good working majority it will be able to do the things which it believes to be for the public interest, instead of having to purchase such a majority by concessions to the separate interests of small groups. When it ceases to command a majority the power can at once pass into the hands of the other party; with some change in policy and personnel, but without interruption of the work of government as a whole. If the Cabinet is the accredited agent of a parliamentary majority, as in England or France at the present day, things will probably work somewhat more smoothly than if they are artificially kept together by the agency of a party organization which controls the machinery of nomination, as did those of eighteenth century England or nineteenth century America. But these are minor differences. The important thing for the maintenance of the system is that there should be two well-defined parties. If there are, one or the other of them will find some means to keep government going and can be held responsible for keeping it on a right course; if there are not, there is perpetual danger that government will drift, for lack of any power strong enough to coordinate the separate forces by which it is moved.

It is precisely this danger with which democratic government has been brought face to face by modern economic conditions—the danger that the system of collective bargaining in politics, known as the *block* system, may render the continued existence of our former parliamentary methods impossible.

When any group of men within the nation has a group interest—usually an economic interest—which its members want to secure at almost any price, and for whose realization they are prepared to sacrifice the national ideas and policies for which their party stands, the character of parliamentary government changes at once. For if such a group holds the balance of power it is no longer possible for the leaders of either party to appeal to a majority in Parliament or in Congress for the support of the measures which they desire to carry out. While they are in power they are at the mercy of a minority; and if they go out of power the leaders of what was formerly the opposition will be no better off than they were. An administration belonging to either party will be compelled to buy support by consenting to measures devised by an organized clique. The most successful statesman will be the one who can keep the largest block—or group of blocks—of votes together at the least sacrifice of principles.

Both in America and in England this change has come upon us somewhat unawares. It may therefore be instructive to trace something of the way in which successive economic groups have arisen in America which have proved strong enough to break down party lines, and to threaten the very existence of what Dicey calls the custom of the constitution, if not of the constitution itself.

The first of these economic groups to make its influence felt in politics was the group of slave-holders. When the United States constitution was adopted most of the leaders of public opinion in Virginia and North Carolina, no less than in New York or Massachusetts, disapproved of negro slavery on principle, and believed that it would gradually die out. Only in the extreme South was there much real sentiment in favour of slavery as an institution. But as time went on the invention of the cotton gin gave the slave-owners unexpected profits. They were enabled to live on large plantations in semi-feudal style and to develop a social life different from that of the North and in some important respects more attractive. Attacks on slavery began to seem like attacks on this social system and attempts to substitute another which they did not like. For many years what they chiefly asked was immunity from these attacks; and so long as they confined themselves to this they were quite content to act with the party of states-rights—the Democratic party as it was called—which could be trusted to protect them from encroachments on their local autonomy. Its principles gave what they wanted, while those of the party of centralization—the so-called Whig party—did not; and therefore the existence of an organized block of slave-holders did not interfere with the operation of the party system. But the time came when they wanted more than protection from encroachments. From 1830 to 1860 the free North was growing so much faster than the slave-owning South that the slave-owners wanted slavery *extension* under national authority. This the Democratic party could not give without violating its own principles. The Northern Democrats led by

Stephen Douglas said that the inhabitants of each territory were the people to decide whether it should come into the Union as a free state or a slave state. The Southern leaders had the choice between remaining in Congress and trying to organize new party groupings—as a modern block would have done—or seceding. Somewhat unwisely they chose the latter method. Far more unwisely they took the initiative in a resort to armed force, and were beaten. The real test of the operation of the American constitution under the block system was thus deferred for many years.

A second economic block which became strong enough to threaten party lines was the high-tariff group whose centre was found in Pennsylvania. This group identified itself with the Whig party almost as naturally as the slave-holding group identified itself with the Democrats; for a protective tariff, as distinct from the tariff for revenue only, was an exercise of national power and a denial of the claim of separate states to develop their own industries in their own way. But there were some protectionists in the Democratic party as well as in the Republican; and in the years following the Civil War it was an embarrassment to party leaders on both sides that their high-tariff men would throw party affiliations overboard to secure high duties on articles produced in their districts or to oppose bills which reduced such duties.

No small part of the mistakes in American tariff legislation was due to the fact that where party strength in Congress was equally divided it became necessary to bid for the support of a tariff block which placed loyalty to the demands of the district above party allegiance.

Still graver dangers were introduced in the period of deflation which followed the Civil War by the protests of the debtor classes against the return to a gold standard. From 1867 to 1877 they demanded increased issues of irredeemable paper; for thirty years more they urged the free coinage of silver. But these movements were somewhat lacking in organization; and, though the inflationists won some notable victories in Congress and in the nominating conventions, when the issue was squarely presented before the people at a general election the importance of maintaining good credit proved a stronger argument with which to appeal to voters than the advantage of paying debts in cheaper money.

The first real sign of breakdown of the American party system came in the reaction against trusts at the beginning of the present century. From 1899 to 1904 the organization of capital in large units resulted in economies of production and distribution that seemed likely to make all classes richer. But it soon appeared that a relatively small number of promoters got the lion's share of the gain. A reaction

set in, which took the form of a movement for extension of government activity in behalf of a "square
deal"; and a "progressive" movement of importance
was organized among younger men in American
politics. This progressive movement was not in itself
of the nature of a block; it was a genuine attempt
to form a new party by those who had a different
view of the American constitution, and different ideas
of the direction which American politics ought to
take, from the somewhat old-fashioned men by whom
both Republican and Democratic parties had been
controlled. Theodore Roosevelt in spite of his age
and his affiliations was in thorough sympathy with a
large part of the ideas which underlay this movement,
and so long as he was President he avoided a break.
He did this partly by his personal ascendancy over
the Progressive leaders and partly by compelling the
Republican party machine to do certain things which
it would much rather have left undone. The actual
split in the Republican party did not take place till
late in Mr Taft's administration; its results were seen
in the election of President Wilson in 1912. For the
first two years he enjoyed the support of a Congressional majority so large that it made no difference
whether he had to face one opposition party or two;
after those two years were over the advent of war
problems—not to speak of those of suffrage and pro-
hibition—tended to distract public attention from

issues on which the Progressives had made their appeal. Under these circumstances the Progressive party, as an organization, broke up; and before the close of Mr Wilson's term of office, its members had generally drifted back to their old allegiance as Republicans or Democrats.

But the old parties, after the war, could not dominate politics as they had done before it. Though the Republican party nominally has a working majority in both Houses of Congress, the majority will not work together as it would of old. For the differences of principle which parties represent are no longer large enough or well enough defined to be of great interest to the voters; and these voters and their representatives are more concerned with pushing the claims of their several localities or classes. This leaves the field free for the block system to operate.

There are three main economic groups or blocks which are putting pressure on members of Congress: the tariff block, the farm block, and the labour block. The first is composed of the old protectionist elements; the second depends for its chief support upon the elements which in the nineteenth century favoured inflation—at that time mostly debtors, now small independent landowners. The labour block is newer and less fully organized; and as far as control of votes is concerned, it seems weaker than either of the others. It might therefore seem to the superficial observer as though there had been little change from the nine-teenth century situation. But the actual problem which confronts Harding is radically different from that which confronted Cleveland or McKinley: not so much because the pressure of divergent economic interests has become stronger, as because the old constitutional differences of opinion, which kept members loyal to their parties in times of crisis, have become very much weaker. "National unity" is no longer a word for the Republican to conjure with; "States Rights" is equally powerless in the mouth of the Democrat. Under such circumstances com-petition between two parties for the suffrage of the people as a whole gives place to bargains with repre-sentatives of separate interests.

The experience which I have described is not peculiar to the United States. It is one which France and Germany have shared; it is one which England is beginning to share in some degree. But there are several reasons which render it less immediately dangerous in Europe than it is in America. In France and in Germany there is—or was until the passing phase of post-war madness set in—a general habit of deferring to expert opinion and especially to the expert opinion of public officials, which sets limits to the power of the legislature to upset the mechanism of government at the behest of private interests. And further, in both France and Germany, the fear of the other nation has always been a potent force to make people sink their private differences when the efficiency of their administration was threatened. Under such circumstances discordant elements have somehow been made to work together by continental statesmen with surprisingly small concession to separate interests.

England has no such protection as France or Germany in these respects; but she has other safeguards of the kind which America sorely lacks. First and most obvious, her old parties have not lost their vitality. Conservative and Liberal are names which stand for a difference of principle in a way which Republican and Democrat have ceased to do. They represent different ways of looking at the present constitution of England and the political future of the Empire, which are important enough to bind the members of each party together amid divergences of economic interest which might otherwise draw them apart. Another less obvious but at least equally important safeguard is found in the traditions of Parliament itself. Parliament was not in its origin a representative body, but, as its name implies, a body for public discussion of national questions; and though it has recently become to all intents and purposes as truly representative as the American Congress or the French Chambers, it retains, in its ethics and in its usages, the stamp set by an older period. Its speeches are still appeals to British public sentiment as a whole. Its members, with few exceptions, still regard themselves as trustees in behalf of the commonwealth, rather than as agents of the particular locality or interest to which they owe their election.

Yet even in England the partial breakdown of party lines in the great war has furnished a premonition of the danger of collective bargaining in politics; and has given us warning that the system of representative government, which was once thought to be the bulwark of civil liberty against privilege, may be used as a cover for assaults by new forms of privilege upon the liberties which our fathers have acquired. When people are taking thought for the public interest, Parliamentary government is probably the best government in the world. When large groups of people are concerned for their own several group interests and let the public interest fall into the background, it may prove the very worst.

And everywhere, even in England, one of the two safeguards which have protected Parliament from the dangers of the block system seems likely to grow weaker. Society and politics are everywhere becoming so far democratic that the differences of principle between Conservative and Liberal are likely to become less potent motives of action than the differences of industrial interest between different localities and different classes in the community. To leave these industrial differences, and the disputes which arise out of them, to settle themselves without government action, as we tried to do in the nineteenth century, seems impossible in the face of the modern tendency toward industrial combination. But to let industrial disputes be decided by a body which is itself little better than an arena of industrial dispute, is to let the blind lead the blind. A conception of politics which would enable a group to hold up the government of the nation while it bargains with the public for a price, is even more monstrously impossible than a system of economics which would allow the nation to be deprived of coal or light or transport for some similar purpose.

A clear-headed nineteenth century observer—Edward John Phelps, for some time American minister to England—was so impressed with these dangers as to say to his friends that the future of popular government seemed to him to depend upon the abolition of legislation by representative assembly. I should myself prefer to say that it was bound up with a maintenance of the sense of trusteeship among members of such assemblies; and that each new development in this twentieth century emphasized the importance of preserving among the members of every legislative assembly those high traditions of trusteeship of which England's Parliaments have given us an example in times past. On this we must rely while we are gradually educating the voter to a similar sense of trusteeship, which is essential to the maintenance of any true democracy under modern conditions.

NATIONAL ANIMOSITY

I HAVE said in a previous lecture that every economic problem in a democracy is to a very large extent a problem in psychology. The statesman has to determine, not simply what is good business for the nation, but how he can persuade the voters, or a majority of them, that it *is* good business. And the latter half of his task is usually harder than the former. For the voter who has been brought up to think that good business means enlightened pursuit of self-interest, tends to apply this standard to matters of public business as well as private; to look, first and foremost, at the question how any proposed measure affects him personally; and if it has, or appears to have, an adverse effect upon his own interests, to be rather blind to the arguments in its favour which can be urged from the public standpoint.

This is particularly true of international problems as distinct from purely national ones. As long as we are dealing with what goes on inside the boundaries of a single country, we can use objective economic reasoning with considerable effect. If we can show a group of workmen that a proposed increase of wages will leave no profit for capital, we can often make them see that it will be suicidal for them to press their demands. If we can show the members of a community that owes money how legislation which is intended to relieve them of the burden of paying part of their debt will have the effect of destroying commercial credit, we can often make them see that they have more to lose than to gain by such legislation. The presidential campaign of 1896 in the United States was actually fought and won by McKinley against Bryan on this purely intellectual ground. But when it comes to international questions it is hard to get the citizen to identify his own interests with those of the foreigner by any means so ineffective as mere reasoning. The world of foreign countries looks pretty far off. It is not easy for an American inexperienced in business to realize how financial troubles in Europe can have any particular effect in his home town. "What have we to do with 'abroad'?" said a Congressman once on the floor of the House of Representatives of the United States; and in so saying I have no doubt that he voiced the instinctive attitude of many of his constituents. And this feeling frequently goes beyond mere indifference. No matter how clearly the statesman can prove that it is for the interest of each nation to have its neighbours prosperous, the majority of his fellow countrymen will be likely to view their neighbours' prosperity with somewhat jealous eyes. The world for which each man really lives is a very small part of the whole world. We have been making some progress in knowledge of what our neighbours are doing; but we have made little or no progress in really caring for them, or in wanting to make their interests our interests and their thoughts our thoughts sufficiently to form a basis of true understanding or of lasting peace.

In fact, there are some important respects in which we have gone backward rather than forward during the last hundred years. In the early part of the nineteenth century there was a tendency among political thinkers to treat the world as a unit, and to assume that the prosperity of each of its several parts contributed to the prosperity of the whole. And in this respect the orators followed the thinkers. They appealed more to the general good of mankind than they do today and less to the special interest of the class or community which their audience represented. Even though the appeals themselves were often fallacious or hypocritical, the fact that they were so habitually put in this form was a good thing for the people and a good sign of the times.

For this cosmopolitan attitude was in line with the whole social and economic philosophy of our grandfathers. If you had once accepted the principle that free competition within your own borders secured such a division of labour that each man did what he could do best and got a fair price for it—giving the community the maximum product, and each individual his proper share—it was but a short step further to say that free immigration from foreign countries simply helped this process of adjustment, and that free trade with other countries extended it to include the whole world. And there were two special reasons which made this way of looking at things popular and acceptable at the beginning of the nineteenth century. The first was that the eighteenth century had seen so much of the evils of restriction in trade and in migration and in choice of occupation, and had had so little opportunity to test the practical effects of freedom, that restriction seemed wholly bad and freedom wholly good. The second was that eighteenth century fortunes had been made in trade rather than by any of the investments of fixed capital which have become the chief source of private wealth in modern times; so that, a hundred years ago, opportunities for free intercourse between nations represented chances to make money for the practical man as well as goals of world policy for the idealist.

Under the combined action of all these influences, the half century which followed the close of the Napoleonic wars witnessed a remarkable breaking down of barriers between the different peoples of the world. In the seventeenth and the eighteenth centuries there had been a tendency on the part of every nation to prohibit emigration, to try to confine its own commerce to its own ships by navigation acts, and to subject imports from foreign countries to very high "protective" taxes. In the nineteenth century all these rigours of this "mercantile" system of political economy were mitigated until the system itself seemed on the point of abandonment. Laws to prevent the free migration of labourers or capitalists from one place to another were either repealed or so administered as to be virtually a dead letter. Laws intended to give each nation a monopoly of its own carrying trade were gradually done away with through the operation of a system of naval reciprocity introduced by Huskisson a century ago. Under this system, if England concluded a reciprocity treaty with Holland, it meant that English ships had the same trading privileges in Dutch ports that they had in English ports and *vice versa*. The practical effect of such a treaty was that ships plying between the two countries could carry cargoes both ways instead of only one way; and the good resulting from this was so great that by the middle of the nineteenth century the world had abandoned the idea on which the old navigation acts were based. There was everywhere a tendency to promote commerce by a lowering of the duties on imports; and England had become definitely committed to the policy of free trade. The time seemed ripe for the extension of that principle to the whole

world; and in 1860 Cobden and Chevalier arranged
a reciprocity treaty between England and France
which had this avowed purpose in view.

The thing that distinguished this commercial treaty
from those which had preceded was the fact that the
reductions of duty which it carried with it were not
sought as special and exclusive privileges for any one
or two nations, but were intended to become part of
a system by which the whole world would benefit.
It was contemplated that both England and France
would make similar treaties with other nations, and
in view of this it was provided that in case either of
the contracting powers should subsequently grant to
a third power conditions more favourable in any
respect than those of this first treaty, the other should
have the benefit of those conditions. This provision
constituted what was known as the "most favoured
nation" clause; it had occasionally been incorporated
into previous treaties, but under the influence of
England and France it now became a habitual part
of every commercial treaty and assumed new and
vastly increased importance by being treated as an
instrument of world-policy. A special concession
made to any one nation now inured at once to the
benefit of a number of others. Belgium aligned herself with France and England in adopting this policy
in 1861, Prussia in 1862, Italy and Spain in 1863.
Practically all nations of Europe except Russia ac-

cepted the principle on which these treaties were based before the close of 1866; and within ten years it seemed to be firmly established as an integral part of sound foreign policy and to ensure steady progress in the direction of free trade.

As a result of all these movements people not only travelled more and traded more, but knew more of each other's powers and capacities. We seemed in 1860 to have entered on an era of mutual understanding and of intelligent division of labour between different parts of the world which would be the surest guarantee of peace. Unfortunately several conditions changed just at the moment when the triumph of Cobden's ideas seemed complete; and a reaction set in, which has continued to the present day, and of which the recent war was a natural and almost inevitable culmination. This reaction was due to a combination of three causes.

In the first place the enormous growth of factories and of other forms of fixed capital made industrial enterprise a very much more important element in the world's business, and left commerce, particularly foreign commerce, a less dominant position than it had hitherto enjoyed. The development of manufactories and of internal transportation took a larger place in the public imagination as a means of increasing national wealth than did foreign trade or the mercantile marine.

In the second place, the results of the operation of large units of fixed capital in factories or railroads led people to doubt whether free competition could be so fully realized or would work so smoothly and fairly as Adam Smith and Ricardo had supposed. And if the principle of competition between individuals did not ensure the results in the home market which its advocates had so confidently predicted, what guarantee had we that the application to international trade would secure better results in the foreign market? So people argued; or rather, so people *felt*, and their feelings were more potent than any argument possibly could have been.

In the third place, the knowledge which different nations gained of one another through immigrants, travellers, or traders, did not have as unmixedly good results as the advocates of freedom had supposed it would. Actual contact with men of other races undoubtedly has a broadening effect, but it also has a disillusioning effect. Whether the chief effect upon us is a gain in breadth or a loss in illusions will depend partly upon the kind of foreigners with whom we come into contact, and partly upon the kind of people we are ourselves. Now neither the average tourist nor the average immigrant comes in contact with the best people of the country he goes to; nor is he fitted to contribute much to mutual understanding, if he did. His language and his thoughts are so far different from those of the country he visits, that it may take many years before understanding takes the place of misunderstanding. Nor is the influence of the trader much better in these respects than that of the traveller; for while he knows far more of what he sees than does the traveller, the use which he makes of his knowledge does not always commend him or his nation to the country of which he is a temporary resident. Thus the net result of universal contact thus far has been to intensify international annoyances rather than to remove them.

To complicate the situation still further, this contact has been followed by a growth of racial consciousness and racial pride—not to say racial prejudice—which is one of the most dangerous elements in the world's present outlook. The character of the danger has been well set forth by Mr Clutton-Brock in a recent article in the *Atlantic Monthly* entitled "Pooled Self-Esteem." Each man, says Mr Clutton-Brock, has a craving for that most delightful possession of the human race, the consciousness of superiority. He longs to think himself wiser, stronger, and more successful than his neighbours. But in nineteen cases out of twenty the facts are too obviously against him if he tries to get personal comfort in this way. He therefore takes refuge in the belief in a *collective* sense of superiority; in the idea that he is one of a nation whose members are wiser, stronger and more successful than the members of any other nation in the world. He and his neighbours repeat this to one another until they come to believe it as the most assured fact of history.

This form of national self-deceit comes up most easily and goes farthest when nations are organized on lines of racial division. Each nation then has obvious physical differences from its neighbours; and physical differences are an even more potent source of misunderstanding or contempt than intellectual ones. Each is united within itself and separated from its neighbours by barriers of language, and differences of thought that go with differences of speech. Each has race traditions of its own, and a racial mythology of its own. Under such conditions the chance for the growth of pooled self-esteem reaches its maximum and the possibility of disillusionment by any means short of wars of extermination is reduced to a minimum.

On the continent of Europe these things have become decisive factors in international politics. For the situation on the continent is such that politicians have constantly been tempted to use race conscious-ness and race prejudice for their own personal ends, and to intensify it in so doing until patriotism took the character of religious fanaticism. When a large part of the members of any race occupies a tolerably well defined territory, there is nothing which gives a political leader so much strength as an appeal to race prejudice. Such an appeal helps him in two ways. It makes him popular because everybody likes to be told that his race is braver and stronger than any other race in the world. It enables him to push his claims and his measures with the utmost force because the sense of racial superiority which he has fostered blinds the people to the dangers involved in his proposals.

The power thus obtained by the demagogue may be used for the most diverse purposes and under the most varied forms. It may be made a weapon for consolidation in Germany or in Italy, for secession in Bohemia or in the Balkans. It may be used for good ends, like those of Cavour, or for a complex mixture of good and bad ends like those of Bismarck, or for wholly bad ends like those of the modern German militarist. It may serve the turn of a monarchist like Napoleon III or of a democrat like Lenin. Wherever it is possible for a leader to invoke race prejudice in support of the line of national policy which he represents he is apt to get the power which he covets, and may succeed in carrying out the policies which he has advocated; but unless he dies in the happy moment of his triumph, like Cavour, he becomes unable to control the ideas and the forces which have placed him in office; and is faced by the alternative of retaining his judgment at the sacrifice of his authority—as did Bismarck—or of retaining his authority at the sacrifice of his judgment—as did Napoleon III or William II.

When President Wilson—whose aims have generally been high, but whose practical measures have not always been well adapted for reaching the end in view—undertook to establish a league of nations based upon the principle of racial self-determination, he seemed to many of us to be making the same kind of mistake which he made in dealing with the railroads and the labour unions of the United States. He tried in either case to introduce the principle of collective bargaining without the safeguards in the way of mutual understanding which are needed to make collective bargaining a success either in industry or in politics. For the arrangement of national boundaries on lines of race tends to lessen points of contact between neighbouring political units; and if each nation is encouraged to settle boundary questions in its own way—which is what racial self-determination means, if it means anything—then "there is always war along the border." There is a popular belief that democracy will prevent such war; but history affords no warrant for this belief. On the whole, democracies seem more likely to misunderstand people of other races than do monarchies, and quicker to proceed to acts of violence on the basis of either real or fancied wrongs. To control a situation like this would have been beyond the power of any league which was primarily a forum for public discussion rather than a centre of executive authority.

Fortunately for Great Britain and for the United States, the national sentiment of patriotism in these countries has not been intensified by racial consciousness and racial illusions to anything like the degree that it was in Germany or in Russia. Neither of the two great English-speaking nations traces its whole ancestry to any one race. The use of the English language is not co-extensive with any national boundary. Where race questions have entered into the politics of England or America—as they have occasionally, to our great discomfort—they have come up as localized movements affecting a part of the public rather than as national movements affecting the public in general. And when racial antagonisms are at their most acute stage, as in Ireland at the present day, England is able to call on a Celtic prime minister to deal with the manifestations of Celtic feeling; no mean advantage as events have more than once proved. Under these circumstances economic considerations as distinct from racial prejudices have probably played a larger proportionate part in determining the policy of England and of America toward their neighbours than has been the case with any nation on the continent of Europe.

I shall try to trace the effect of these economic considerations on the international policy of the United

States; to show how, under the combined influence of the three factors I have named—increase of fixed capital, diminished reliance on free competition, and growth of national feeling—the mental attitude of the American citizen on questions of immigration, protective tariffs, or foreign commerce changed from the broad liberalism of 1860, whose development I described in an earlier lecture, to the more exclusive nationalism of 1920; and to indicate some of the dangers to which this reaction has laid us open.

The original attitude of the American public toward the immigrant was one of hearty welcome. Part of this cordiality was due to immediate political and social conditions—to the fact that the country would be stronger for defence against European nations, particularly against Spain in the Southwest, if it were more thickly settled, and to the fact that land was so abundant that the law of diminishing return had not begun to operate, and more labour meant more product *per capita* instead of less. But a part, and probably a large part, was due to a general acceptance of the idea of *fraternity* along with liberty and equality as an essential feature of democracy. The Jeffersonian Democrats believed that restraints upon individual freedom, class distinctions, and national antagonisms, were elements of an artificial system, whereby the natural good impulses of the human soul were hampered; and they were ready to welcome everyone, without regard to his previous training, to full enjoyment of civil and political liberty as an American. As most of the Democratic strength lay among the masses rather than among the property owners, this belief in fraternity ensured a cordiality to the immigrant in quarters where hostility might otherwise have been expected—among those with whom he competed as distinct from those for whom he worked.

From this general welcome two classes only were excluded—the Indian and the Negro. But neither of these classes was composed of immigrants in the proper sense of the word. Perhaps if they had been, they would have stood a better chance of being welcomed. Unfortunately the settlers had already come to know them so well that they saw, and even exaggerated, the qualities which would prevent them from making self-governing citizens until they had changed a good deal. The Indian had been hated as an enemy; the Negro had been looked down upon as a slave. Under these circumstances Americans shrunk from extending the idea of fraternity so wide as to include in their civic brotherhood men so cruel as the Indian had proved himself, or so servile as the Negro had appeared. But, so far as actual immigrants were concerned, the strength and universality of the sentiment of fraternity were remarkable. In certain quarters there was some apprehension of danger from the large influx of Catholics; but this arose simply from fear that the Church as an organization would menace free thought and prevent its members from becoming a part of the American commonwealth in such a way as to get the full benefit of free institutions.

Until after the Civil War America had no doubt of her capacity to assimilate all immigrants politically and to profit by them economically if she were only given a fair chance. But about 1870 the increase of Chinese immigration in the West and of "assisted" immigration in the East awakened men's minds to possible dangers of which they had not previously thought.

Industrially the Chinese who came to America were highly efficient. They produced a great deal and lived on very little. They were formidable competitors, and they were not profitable customers. They threatened to bring wages down in the lines in which they were employed without making new openings for labour in other lines. We could not assimilate them politically because they did not wish to be assimilated. Nearly all of them regarded their stay in America as transient. Most of their savings were sent back to China instead of being invested in the United States. The Chinese tended to form alien communities in our Western States, with systems of morals different from our own, whose evils were only too obvious, and whose merits we could not appreciate.

A somewhat similar situation had arisen in the

East in a different fashion. In the years following the Civil War a number of concerns had imported labourers "under contract,"—paying their passage money as an advance on an agreement that the immigrant would work for them after his arrival for a specified time and under specified conditions. The case of these contract labourers differed in some respects from that of the Chinese. They were not so efficient and therefore not such dangerous competitors. They spent their money more freely, and made better customers for the local tradesmen. As a rule they intended to stay in America and were anxious to learn American ways. But the fact remained that they were imported by employers to keep labour cost down, and that with all their anxiety to become Americans, they did not learn our language or our habits of thought with the rapidity which the independent immigrants had done. They remained for some time, like the Chinese, alien elements in our midst.

Employers of contract labour in the East and of Chinese labour in the West contended that these dangers were largely imaginary; that cheap labour meant high profits, and that these profits when reinvested meant added employment for labour under good conditions. When representatives of organized labour in 1875 or 1880 argued for restriction of immigration on one set of economic grounds, representatives of organized capital argued against it on another set of grounds, which were at least equally plausible. This was the time and manner in which the labour question first came into American politics. Had the issue been decided by purely economic arguments, victory would almost certainly have gone to the employers; for at that time an overwhelming majority of American voters either owned invested property or expected to do so, and were inclined to look at economic questions from the capitalistic standpoint. But the political and social dangers of unrestricted immigration turned the victory in the other direction. The entry of Chinese labourers was suspended in 1882, and was subsequently prohibited. When the Japanese began to come in considerable numbers, the same policy was applied to Japan. Immigration under contract in the form which I have described was made unlawful in 1885, and the restriction has been extended and made more stringent by subsequent acts.

This change had an importance and a significance of which few of us dreamed at the time. It represented the introduction of a new principle into American politics and a new theory into national legislation—the theory that the maintenance of the standard of living of the American workman and of the integrity of American ideals depended on Acts of Congress. It represented a definite renouncement of the hopes of the founders of the republic regarding individual liberty and individual initiative. It has had a marked effect on all subsequent discussion of the tariff and of foreign trade. And it is the source of a large part of the difficulty which American financiers and statesmen today encounter in dealing with world problems of reconstruction.

Down to the time of the Civil War the American tariff of duties on imports had been generally arranged with the idea of producing the necessary revenue for the government with the least disturbance of trade. As we had no national income tax during those years, and people did not want to have one, the tariff rates were sometimes put fairly high, and gave a good deal of incidental protection; but, except for certain short periods, revenue rather than protection had been the dominant purpose. And those who argued most actively for protection wanted it as a means of diversifying industry and urged it on that ground. The abundance of free land made American wages high. It was *because* of these high wages that the manufacturers asked protection in order that America might capitalize her savings as buildings and machinery instead of exhausting her national resources and sacrificing future strength to present profit. They were for the most part content to ask for temporary protection to "infant industries." I am not concerned with the soundness or unsoundness of their arguments from the economic standpoint; I am simply concerned to show the character of the appeal. It was not in behalf of American labour as against foreign labour, it was avowedly in behalf of one kind of American investment of capital as against another kind.

When the Civil War came, the withdrawal of the cotton states, where the free-trade sentiment had been strongest, gave the protectionists a majority in both houses of Congress; and tariff rates were rapidly raised. Yet the war tariff was primarily a revenue measure; and some of its provisions which ultimately became most burdensome, particularly in the woollen schedules, were imposed as offsets to internal revenue taxes which woollen manufacturers in America had to pay. The real passage to a protective system came in 1867 after the close of the war, when internal revenue taxes were reduced or abolished, and import duties were left almost unchanged. The high and un-equalized protection which was then adopted caused grave dissatisfaction in many quarters. But the primary subject of public interest for more than a decade after the Civil War was the problem of reconstruction in the Southern States; and next in importance came the resumption of specie payments: so that nothing really effective in the way of tariff reform was undertaken by either party for more than fifteen years after the war closed.

During this period a great deal of capital had been invested in industrial enterprises which made a moderate profit under high protection but which would have to close their doors if tariffs were lowered. They were no longer infant industries; their operation was not essential to the business of the country; but their closing would throw a number of people out of work, many of whom would find it hard to get employment. It was on behalf of such workmen that the strongest appeals against tariff reduction were now based. For many years manufacturers had been telling their employees—sometimes with truth— that the tariff was what made *their* wages high. The protectionist leaders now made a much wider use of this appeal and told the American people that the tariff was what made *American* wages high—or at any rate what kept them so; and that if we laid ourselves open to foreign competition our operatives must be prepared to accept foreign wage rates and foreign standards of living.

The strength of a political appeal depends on some other things besides its logical force. This one proved astonishingly strong; strong enough to defeat Grover Cleveland when he was a candidate for re-election in 1888 on the tariff reform issue, and strong enough to secure the return of a high-tariff majority in Congress for more than three-quarters of the time since that date. Its chief strength and its chief significance lie in the fact that it represents a changed attitude on the part of the American people—a change from self-reliance to reliance on government, from belief in open competition to distrust of open competition, from welcoming the foreigner as a customer to fearing the foreigner as a rival or an enemy.

For the change of policy regarding immigration and import duties is the outcome and the symptom of a changed attitude toward foreign trade as a whole. A hundred years ago it was a matter of national ambition and national pride in the United States to get as large a share as possible of the world's commerce. To send goods to the markets where they were wanted, sell them at a profit, and bring back other goods which we could not produce as cheaply as our neighbours, seemed, and generally was, the best way to get rich. It also seemed, and generally was, the best way to keep in touch with the business of the world as a whole; to promote international peace and international understanding by creating a body of common trade interests. Today—I say it with regret—we are apt to look at the matter in another light. We assume a defensive attitude toward world commerce. The first question we ask is "Who is going to be hurt by the imports?" In our anxiety to protect the home producer, we overlook alike the needs of the home consumer and the needs of the export trade. For the sake of a comparatively small industry which we carry on at some disadvantage—like the growth of lemons, for instance, which is rendered precarious by frost—we have subjected the users of lemons to a heavy tax, and have deprived Mediterranean countries of one of their best means of trading with us. The theory of the protective system as held by its advocates in the United States today is that the tariff on every article which we can produce should be made at least high enough to offset the difference in labour cost in the country of origin and our own—in other words, to confiscate all the profit to the importer, except on a few articles which we cannot produce at all. Matters do not always go quite so far as this in practice; the adverse effect on the public revenue would be too great. But there are a great many Americans, both in Congress and out of it, who accept the protective theory as I have given it and regard any departure from it as a misfortune. And this has the effect of making them indifferent or hostile to the measures which are needed to put our foreign trade on a sound basis. They want us to have exports; but when we ask how the foreigner is to pay for his exports when he has hardly any gold left, and we are not quite ready to give him any more credit, they have no answer, except to talk of subsidies for shipping. And subsidies for shipping will not make trade unless you are prepared to take some means of payment which the foreigner has to offer.

I shall not attempt to discuss the economic loss which America herself has suffered from this development of the protective theory. I prefer to lay emphasis on the evils and dangers in the way of international misunderstanding to which America has exposed herself, and to which other democracies are likely to be exposed if they model their tariff policy upon ours.

In the first place, their statesmen and their financiers are hampered in all attempts to deal with international questions of trade, currency, and credit. Their hands are tied by the fact that a large part of the people have been trained to fear foreign imports to such an extent that they judge all these questions short-sightedly. We cannot make arrangements for Europe to pay her debts to us so long as we object to receiving three-quarters of the articles in which she would naturally pay them. We cannot, as our recent experience shows, get profitable trade with South America or Asia by mere increase of credit facilities. The question how the credit can be liquidated is even more important than the question how it can be created. And any promising plan of liquidation seems to involve freer welcome to foreign goods than the American public has been willing to accord.

In the next place, continuance of this policy means commercial isolation. If other democracies follow the lead of the United States in trying to produce everything within their own borders and in using the tariff as a defensive weapon to make this possible, we shall see the overthrow of nearly everything which was accomplished during the earlier part of the nineteenth century to bring nations closer together. Democracy will set the seal of permanence on the destructive work of the Hohenzollerns. The one hope of accord between nations is that they shall be willing to deal with one another commercially on a fair basis; that each people shall view its neighbours as possible customers to be attracted and not simply as possible rivals to be kept at a distance.

For a policy of commercial isolation vastly increases the danger of war. It engenders a spirit of distrust which can easily break out in actual manifestation of hostility; it prevents the establishment of those common business interests which constitute the only real obstacle to actual fighting when antagonistic feeling has been once aroused. Anyone who has attended meetings of workmen is familiar with the phrase so constantly heard in such gatherings that wars are brought about by capital. The truth or falsehood of this statement depends on the national attitude towards foreign trade. If foreign trade is regarded as a contest, capital goes into warlike channels; if foreign trade is regarded as a means of mutual advantage and as an extension of the principle of division of labour to include nations as well as individuals, invested capital is the surest guardian of the peace.

And if war does come, it takes the commercially isolated people at a disadvantage. The nations which have developed their foreign trade intelligently, promoting exports of some things by welcoming imports of others, have put themselves in a position to stand together; those which have killed their foreign trade in order to make some of their industries independent of foreign competition, have put themselves in a position to fall separately. Commercial isolation under present world conditions represents a purely *defensive* economic policy, dictated by timidity. It seldom happens that a purely defensive policy succeeds, either in peace or in war, when others are prepared to pursue an aggressive one; it is still more rare to find timidity a match for courage. Among all the dangers to which modern democracy is liable I count this recent extension of the protective theory the gravest. Among all the problems which confront its leaders, I count as most vital the education of the public to the habit of exercising foresight and courage in dealing with international affairs.

CLASS CONSCIOUSNESS AND
PUBLIC OPINION

WE have seen in previous lectures that the strength of a modern state depends on its success in solving its industrial problems—in other words, upon getting its work done efficiently and progressively. In the case of any true democracy or government by the people, this must be accomplished, not by compulsion, but by a call to which the people will respond of their own independent volition. The founders of the American commonwealth thought that they could accomplish it by an appeal to the self-interest of each individual; by giving each man as good a chance as possible to acquire property, and as much freedom as possible in investing what he had acquired. They held that the competition among the members of each industrial class or group would be sufficient to prevent that group from making unfair profits and pursuing its own industrial interests at the expense of those of the nation.

In the early part of the nineteenth century it seemed quite possible to secure these conditions and these results. But in the latter part of the century production and transportation developed in such a way that competition in many lines of industry was no longer practicable—partly because a single group of factories or a single telephone system could do the work cheaper than several independent concerns, and partly because it could serve the public more effectively than they could. When competition had thus been done away with, the protection which the public had enjoyed against unfair rates was also done away with. Powerful group interests were created, whose primary object was to increase their own returns; which not only tried to keep their prices at the maximum figure, but were ready to limit their output as a means to that end.

To protect the community against these dangers men resorted to legislative control. But the result was disappointing. Instead of protecting the public against organized industrial interests, it too often brought the organized influence of such interests into legislative assemblies, to the great detriment of the whole system of representative government and the sacrifice of public well-being. Control of collective bargaining in industry by collective bargaining in politics may sometimes be a necessity; but as a system it promotes neither good business nor good government.

And even worse than the effect of the group system on business or politics, has been its effect on men's character and vision. We hear a great deal in these days about the development of "class consciousness" or "racial solidarity." Few of those who use these words understand what the things themselves really mean or what dangers are involved in their growth. Class consciousness in its early stages means that the members of a social or economic group are so impressed with their own moral superiority to the rest of the community that they care relatively little what the rest of the community thinks or what becomes of it. In its later stages it means that they become so absorbed in the wishes and aspirations of their own group that they mistake these for facts and acquire a mental blindness which prevents them from taking any other kind of facts into account. Racial solidarity is class consciousness applied on a wider scale—"pooled self-esteem" as Mr Clutton-Brock so aptly calls it. The more this class consciousness is developed the harder it will be for democracy to deal with internal politics; the more this racial solidarity is developed, the harder it will be for it to deal with international politics. For if the people are to govern, the people must see facts as they really are.

Some observers regard this growth of class conflicts and race conflicts as a relapse of mankind into a state of selfishness and lawlessness from which the world had partially emerged; and believe that the evil is so deep-seated as to require a new religion—or a revival of the old religion—to cure it. But, cordially as I should welcome any increase of the religious spirit, under old forms or new ones, I cannot concur in these views as to the seat of the evil or the kind of remedy which is most immediately needed. I can see no evidence that the present chaotic state of industry and politics is due to an increase in selfishness in the community as a whole. Never was there a time when people were more ready to sacrifice their own comfort and their own independence when there was a clear public duty to do so. If we want proof of this, we need only to look back at the history of volunteering in England and of conscription in America during the last war. The Germans thought that men who had been accustomed to be guided by self-interest and to be impatient of government authority would neither volunteer as individuals to endure the hardships of military life for the benefit of the commonwealth nor accept the collective obligation of compulsory service. But the Germans were wrong in both these predictions. When people saw a clear public duty before them, most of them were ready to set selfish considerations of personal comfort and personal independence aside. The more terrible the Germans made war, the clearer was the public duty and the ampler the self-sacrifice. Of course there were many individuals both in England and in America who showed quite a different spirit— profiteers or adventurers, in business or in politics, who sought only to make their own market out of the nation's troubles. But such men were few in number as compared with the whole body of freemen.

Now what was true in war is true in peace. The masses of people are essentially sound at heart. It is not from lack of patriotism or public spirit that they fail to make the same kind of sacrifices in peace that they did in war; it is because they fail to see the need of applying their patriotism and public spirit in matters of business.

And no wonder that they fail to see it. For three generations we have been teaching a philosophy of business that was, fundamentally, an appeal to self-interest. We have been resting comfortably in the belief that if each man was encouraged to pursue his own ends in a clear-headed way, competition would secure efficiency in production and just distribution of rewards. Now this was never wholly true—selfish people were never quite clear-headed enough to make the theory work out as it should, and were continually doing inefficient or unjust things from stupidity or shortsightedness; but with the amount of competition which prevailed in the first half of the nineteenth century, it came tolerably near being true. With the progress of industrial consolidation in the latter half of the nineteenth century it has ceased to be true, even in this rough way. We have just learned to face this as an economic fact; we have not yet faced its ethical consequences. Nearly everybody sees how this change affects his business methods and understands that his own success today is quite as apt to depend on advantages in collective bargaining as on success in competition. Very few understand how this change affects their duties toward the public, and makes it unsafe to apply an old code of business morals to new industrial problems. Success in competition is usually won by public service—increased production at minimum cost. Success in collective bargaining is usually won at public expense—limited production at maximum cost. A degree of selfishness in business transactions which under nineteenth century conditions was safe and generally advantageous for the community has become under twentieth century conditions unsafe and generally disastrous. Can these facts be brought home to the people as a whole in such a way that they will act upon them? Can they be made to understand that in the keen industrial struggle between modern communities selfish interference with work may be as ruinously unpatriotic as selfish unwillingness to fight?

The difficulty is an intellectual rather than a moral one. Our fundamental problem, as leaders of democracy, is to make people see what really is their duty under modern conditions, instead of letting them think they are doing their duty in applying yesterday's ideals of morals and of law to the business of today. We have a double task before us—to frame a new system of ethics which shall keep nations sound and strong after competition has been abandoned or limited, and to educate the public to accept this new system and the obligations which it imposes.

To build up a new system we generally have to begin by clearing out some of the deadwood of the old system; and the case in hand is no exception. We have two large pieces of ethical deadwood to remove; the belief on the part of the capitalists that property right is something sacred and the belief on the part of the workingman that labour creates value.

To some of this audience, the first of these beliefs may not seem to be a very grave obstacle in the way of reform. So many property rights which appeared sacred in mid-Victorian days have been either upset or rendered valueless during recent years, that the property owner's powers of obstruction are reduced to a minimum. But this does not mean that the property owner's mental attitude has changed correspondingly; and as long as the old attitude persists, class misunderstanding will continue and the building up of a new system of ethics to be accepted by the whole community will remain impossible. Property right is not a sacred thing set apart or consecrated as an end in itself. It is an institution which has grown up for the benefit of society as a whole, and taken different forms to meet the needs of different ages. I believe it is generally true that rapid changes in the law of property right are dangerous and quite as apt to hurt society as to help it; but to protest, even in one's own mind, against all change, is to invite rapid change, rather than to hinder it.

In applying the law to any given case, a court is moved by two sets of considerations; the consideration of what has been done in similar cases in the past, and the consideration of what needs to be done under present conditions in order to secure the ends for which government is established. The law, as Mr Justice Cardozo puts it, must hold the traditional and the sociological requirements in proper balance. Throughout the greater part of their history, the English courts have been extremely successful in doing this, and have gradually modified the law of private property, by judicial interpretation and accretion, to meet the varying needs of industry.

But in the last hundred years industrial development has been moving so fast that the English courts have found it hard to keep up with it; and the American courts have apparently found it still harder. The result has been that the community has resorted to its legislative assemblies to get changes in organic law made more promptly than the courts would make them. This has been unfortunate in many ways. A legislature seldom appreciates the indirect results of its action as fully as a court does. In trying to do one good thing that it sees, it opens the way for a number of bad things which it does not see. In meeting the demands of one or more industrial groups which constitute a majority of its members, it may frame a bill in which the interests of an unorganized majority of the people are left almost wholly out of sight. Instead of an orderly development of law as an expression of public opinion, we find a struggle between progressives who carry measures through the legislature regardless of traditional rights, and conservatives who appeal to the courts for defence against the results of such measures, not because they hurt society, but because they violate precedent.

As long as this state of things continues, the building up of a new system of industrial ethics is impossible. Before we can accomplish anything positive, the property owners and their counsel must accept the idea that private property is in the large sense a public trust, and that the rights of the property owner in the courts depend upon the extent to which the perpetuation of the trust contributes to the purposes for which it was created. Thus and thus only do we find common ground on which conservative and progressive can meet and get an understanding of one another's point of view. By giving up the assumption that his property rights are sacred, the property owner puts himself in a position to discuss the question whether they are useful to society; with a good chance of being heard, and a fair chance of being understood by the people as a whole.

The other obstacle which blocks our attempts to secure a consensus of public opinion on industrial questions, and to frame a system of ethics adapted to modern industrial conditions, is the widespread belief in the proposition that labour creates value. As a generalization this is obviously untrue. To say that labour *often* creates value is right. To say that it *ought* to create value may possibly be right; it depends largely upon what the speaker means by the elusive word "ought." But to say that it *does so* as a general proposition—that if A works a day and produces something which B wants, and B works a day and produces something which A does *not* want, the value of the two results is equal—is contrary to the obvious and accepted meaning of the word "value."

The man who did more than anyone else to popularize the labour-value theory—Karl Marx—recognized this fact; and in theoretical discussion he qualified his statement by saying that he referred only to "socially necessary" labour. But in public agitation, which was the thing he had at heart, he and his followers let this qualification slip out of sight. The temptation to do this was very great. Each man likes to think that his work is worth as much as that of anyone else; the question whether other people want what he produces is easily waved away as irrelevant. Outside of England and America the idea that labour is what creates value has become an article of faith among labourers as a body—among a large part of the men and women who are going to be the voters of the world and direct its policies. And in the present tendency of democracy to pursue industrial equality in preference to all other ends—liberty, efficiency, or progress—the belief is as dangerous as it is comfortable. It has formed the basis of the class consciousness of the labourers in the same way that the doctrine of the sacredness of property formed a part of the class consciousness of the property holders a hundred years ago. Under such circumstances, the man who attempts to disprove the theory by direct argument, and show that the value of the product is what gives value to the labour, is at a great disadvantage. Men will sooner distrust logic than doubt an article of faith. Even when the application of the theory brings disaster, as it did in the commercial workshops of Paris in 1848 or in the Soviet regime in Russia in 1921, the Marxian socialist attributes the failure to the mistakes of his leaders or the machinations of his enemies, rather than to any inherent defect in the theory itself.

But it must be met in some way if democracy is to endure. For if people accept the proposition that all value is created by labour, the rest of the Marxian theory follows as a matter of course. Profits are made by buying labour or its immediate products for less than their value and selling them for more than their value; capital is simply the heaped up accumulation of such profits; confiscation of capital by labour is the one logical method to get redress for past wrongs, and secure justice for future generations of labourers. The only way in which the conservative elements in the community can meet this problem is by checking the growth of class consciousness; by preventing the erection of emotional barriers which will hinder free discussion between different elements of the community, and by breaking down as rapidly as possible those which now exist.

Of the means at command, the simplest and most immediately effective is the curtailment of all ostentatious expenditure—of luxury in the ordinary sense. Such expenditure raises barriers between classes in two ways. In the first place the extravagance of those who have property causes envy and bitterness of feeling among those who have none, and makes community of patriotic feeling between the two groups impossible. There is hardly any need of expanding this idea. The first French Revolution was probably due quite as much to the ostentation of the rich as to the pressure of actual misgovernment. Men are readier to endure hardship than to have the difference between themselves and others flaunted in their face.

And in the second place, any ostentation of the

property owner in spending his money leads the labourer to vie with him to the extent of his power whenever he has the chance; in other words to spend his surplus wages instead of saving them. Money that the labourer might have invested in ways that would protect him from want and at the same time give him some understanding of the capitalist's difficulties and just claims is wasted in imitating his extravagances and has no educational effect or else a bad one. The old-fashioned economists were right in condemning luxury; but they failed to put their condemnation on the strongest ground—the influence of example in preventing the diffusion of the habit of saving. If the rich spend money foolishly, it is vain to expect that the poor will be wiser than they.

But it is not enough to exercise moderation in the spending of money; it will be necessary to exercise greater moderation in its pursuit. If business men expect a democratic society to leave them in control of commerce and of manufacture they must learn to give commercial and manufacturing business the character of a profession instead of a trade.

The essential difference between a trade and a profession, as I understand it, is that the man who is engaged in trade feels justified in charging all the market will allow, while the professional man regards himself as being so far a public servant that he is prepared to do his work for less than its market value.

The line between the two is somewhat ill-defined and I am afraid the tendency in recent years has been to shift it in the wrong direction—to commercialize our medicine and our law and our science, rather than to professionalize our business. But with the large careers which modern industry offers to its managers and advisers, I believe that these men would be content to accept a return much lower than the commercial value of their services, if it were understood that they, individually and as a class, would gain in public appreciation by so doing.

For the pursuit of wealth at the present day is not due to avarice, except in very slight degree. It is due to motives of ambition; partly to a desire to win visible evidence of success in a great game, and partly to a wish to secure the power of controlling large industrial forces. And with the best men it is the last motive which really counts. The possession of industrial power and the chance for using it widely and wisely, would be an all-sufficient reward for the business man's ambition, if business became really and truly a profession, in which success was measured by service rendered rather than by money received.

I do not mean to imply that from a strictly commercial standpoint our business men have been overpaid for their services. In the complex conditions of modern industry the danger of producing the wrong thing, or of furnishing a thing at times when it is not wanted, is so enormously great that the men who can foresee what the market is going to need may prevent the waste of millions of days of labour and furnish a product whose utility to society is double or treble its labour cost. The community which forgoes the expense of skilled directors may, and generally does, turn that profit into a loss. To this extent the director of industry may be justified in claiming a large part of the surplus as being properly his work and asking society to recognize that claim. But there are other considerations besides the purely commercial one which should properly appeal to him as a public spirited citizen, and to the publicists who advise him what he ought to do and advise society what it ought to do. His example in charging full commercial value for honest service is an encouragement to every profiteer to charge all he can get for the results of dishonest service or of no service at all. The large fortunes made by him and by the profiteers who are associated with him in the public mind may lead the voters to take control out of his hands and put it into hands which are too unskilled to serve the community properly. For the difference in public service between a man trained in business, foreseeing the wants of the market by intuition, and a government official, trying to draw what inferences he can from statistical reports, is a world-wide one. Under circumstances like these the question of his duty is no longer the private one whether he has given an equivalent for what he has received, but the public one whether he endangers the commonwealth by taking it.

I do not know how it may be in England, but in America there is not a great deal of jealousy of the *power* of the capitalists among the rank and file of the labourers as distinct from the leaders. Whatever their theories, they have sense enough to see that centralization of authority is essential to their own safety as well as to the smooth running of the country; and they are quite content to leave that authority where it stands at present. But there *is* jealousy of the wealth of the capitalist; and in the hope of getting part of that wealth they are willing to back their own leaders in the struggle for control. If the two questions could be separated, I am sure that American labourers as a body would be conservative as regards methods of factory or railway organization; and that we should avoid many of the dangers of premature adoption of state ownership and inefficient management of state-owned industry to which democracies are now exposed.

I am putting this matter on broad grounds, not on narrow ones. I am not urging that capitalists should forgo part of their profits to prevent nationalization of railways or coal mines. This may ultimately come in any event. What concerns me is to prevent railways and mines from getting into the hands of an uneducated public which believes that one man's labour is worth as much as another's. If the voters as a body once learn that value depends upon service to society and that those who direct the labour and capital of the community have to do something more difficult than a mere estimate of costs, they will use the same care in the selection of railway presidents or mine superintendents which they now use in selecting judges; and will not tolerate such mistakes, such inefficiency, and such losses as characterized American railway operation under government hands during the late war.

Two questions will doubtless occur in this connection—what ought to be done with the surplus profit, and how this change of industrial ethics can be brought about. The first of these questions can be answered in so many ways that I am afraid I shall have to pass it over; but the answer to the second is easy and brief. It can be done by public opinion, if the intelligent public once becomes clear as to the necessity. When it was first suggested in America that certain abuses of the corporate trust which the law was powerless to reach could be dealt with by social ostracism, the idea was pronounced absurd and made the subject of cartoons in every comic paper. But greater consequences were produced in that way than by statutes or by dissolution suits.

And apart from the positive results which may be

secured in distributing wealth more equally, the mere change of attitude on the part of property holders will clear the air wonderfully. It will remove all ground for a group of ideas regarding law and law courts which, in America at any rate, are widely prevalent and stand in the way of any orderly system of government by the people.

When the men who control industry regard property as a vested right which they can push to its utmost limits, and rely on the courts for protection in so doing, it is inevitable that the men who do not own property should regard the courts as enemies of progress, and distrust judge-made law as a mere summary of tradition rather than a reasoned statement of what justice requires at the present day. If this distrust is well founded, government by the people in the true sense of the word—government by public opinion duly articulated—ceases to be possible. For there is no longer one coherent public opinion, articulated by the Legislature *and* by the Courts, but two opposing sets of opinions with no adequate agency for reconciling them.

During the greater part of the history of England the courts have in fact acted as such an agency. They have not only administered justice more impartially than was the case on the continent but they have been on the side of industrial progress; using legal fictions, if necessary, to evade the letter of the older law if it became repugnant to justice under newer conditions. Of course there have been some bad judges and some stupid ones; but English judges as a class have been distinguished for political wisdom hardly less than for personal honesty. Above all, they have been a great educational force in English government. They told why they did things in a way that commended their actions to the intelligent public and kept public opinion and law in harmony. Anyone who reads Blackstone's commentaries can see what was the influence and effect of these educational traditions in the eighteenth century.

Just at the close of that century Jeremy Bentham criticized Blackstone, and judges who worked on Blackstone's lines, for treating law as if it were an expression of ideal justice. Law, said Bentham, is what the sovereign commands. The judge's business is, not to find out what the King in Parliament *ought* to have said, but what he *did* say. The court may and should interpret it as equitably as possible in applying it to particular cases; but law is one thing and morals another, and a thing is not law because it commends itself to men's conscience. As a matter of logic Bentham and his followers had the best of the argument; as a matter of political wisdom, the theories of Blackstone were safer to follow. In accepting Bentham's view the nineteenth century courts avoided a good many mistakes of reasoning which their predecessors had committed, and left out some nonsense from their decisions; but they lost a great deal of the direct touch with public opinion which previous generations of judges had enjoyed, and tended to become, in fact as well as in theory, exponents of tradition—letting people look to the legislative branch of the government for progress.

We are today witnessing the beginnings of a strong reaction against Bentham's view. An increasingly large number of judges, both in England and in America, recognize that the court has the double duty of reconciling the claims of past tradition with those of present modes of life. The first effect of this reaction in the United States has not been wholly fortunate. It has had the effect of dividing our courts and increasing the number of dissenting opinions. Where it is a question of applying constitutional principles to industrial problems, the conservatives and the progressives give such different weight to the different elements which enter into the discussion of the case before them that it is often impossible to reach anything like unanimity. But I believe that this is a passing phase; and that the conservatives and progressives on the bench will not only find common ground on which to decide the cases that come before them, but will unite public opinion behind them on the ground thus taken. They will *certainly* do it if the property owners can accept the idea that industrial capital should be regarded as a public trust, in ethics as well as in law.

For the mass of the labourers of England and of America have neither the will nor the power to oppose the development of any system of industrial property right which is based on the needs of the public and appeals to a genuine public opinion. In neither country do the leading workmen deceive themselves with fallacies like those of Karl Marx. In trades where foreigners are numerous or in which discontent has been specially active, communistic sentiments may find ready hearing among the rank and file. But the great majority of able working men are ambitious either to become property holders or to be leaders of a union with a history; and Marxian socialism offers as little promise of success in the one line as in the other.

But there remains an additional step to be taken, in order to equip the public opinion of our democracies for dealing with modern industrial conditions and to do away with the baleful effects of the period of class consciousness through which we are passing. We must make provision for giving the voters as a body the elements of a liberal education in the true sense of the word—an education which fits them for the exercise of *liberty*, civil and political.

This true meaning of a liberal education is so often misunderstood that it will perhaps come as a surprise to some of us to be reminded of it. In contrasting the liberally educated man with the technically educated man, we think of the former as having acquired knowledge and interest in many lines, while the latter confines his knowledge and interest to the few which bear on his profession or trade. But those who take this view miss the essential points and purposes involved. To begin with, education is not, except to a limited extent, an acquiring of knowledge. It is essentially a training of habits and powers. A good deal of knowledge is incidentally acquired in the course of this training; but such knowledge is an incident of the education, not its essential instrument or essential object. The difference between bad and good ideals of education may be summed up by saying that bad education teaches us to know, while good education teaches us to know *how*—how to find things, to judge things, and above all to do things. Technical education trains a man to find and judge and do what is necessary in his calling; liberal education trains him to find and judge and do what is necessary in the exercise of his liberty as a citizen.

The founders of the American commonwealth understood the importance of this sort of liberal education, and the necessity that every one of its members should have some of it in order to be trusted with rights of self-government and a share in the government of the community. One of their very first cares was to provide a system of public education under which every child should learn reading, writing, and arithmetic. This education did not go very far, but it went straight toward the mark. It put in the hands of American children powers that would enable them to take intelligent part in public business when they grew up. It did not undertake to give much knowledge of politics or economics; it left that to be acquired afterwards, in the jury box or the political campaign, from the newspaper or the counting room. For this, it taught them to rely on themselves.

The elementary schools developed under the influence of these ideas and purposes have continued down to the present day to be the most satisfactory part of the American public school system. Speaking broadly, they have given every boy his chance, and have made patriotic Americans out of nineteen-twentieths of the material that came into their hands, even though some of it was very unpromising. Our public high schools are for the most part of later origin and have had a wider aim; but they have not been equally successful in attaining it. They have tried to give the boys and girls who attended them many kinds of knowledge and training which would be interesting to them in school and useful in after life; but they have suffered in their efforts from two disadvantages, which in the state of public feeling at the middle of the last century were almost unavoidable. The first was the over-valuation of mere knowledge as compared with training; almost every parent wanted his boys taught *facts* on the subjects in which he himself was most interested, and was impatient of any educational system which left him ignorant of these facts. The second was the belief encouraged by Herbert Spencer that studies ought to be naturally interesting to the pupil, and the idea, for which it is not fair to hold Spencer responsible, that it was the duty of the teacher to make them so if they were not. Pupils trained under these influences in school or college—for our colleges were not exempt from these adverse influences—gained knowledge rather than power, breadth rather than accuracy or efficiency, habits of dependence rather than habits of self-reliance.

It is this last point which shows the gravest defect of the system from a political standpoint. If breadth is purchased at the expense of self-reliance, the education is an illiberal one—an actual detriment to the exercise of civil liberty. The boy who has become accustomed to depend on the teacher for his knowledge in school tends to take his knowledge at second hand in after life. The boy who can study only what he likes in school is governed in after life by his likes and dislikes rather than by his reason. America is just beginning to see this; and as a consequence we have somewhat better standards of education than we had twenty years ago. I sincerely trust that England, in dealing with her present and prospective problems of national education, may take warning by our mistakes and not feel compelled to repeat them.

If we can once get back to the habit of regarding education as a training in self-reliance, we can accomplish many things which have seemed almost impossible to modern democracy. By putting a proper share of responsibility upon the pupils, we can vastly increase our amount of real teaching without any corresponding increase of cost. By demanding efficiency and accuracy in school we can train our citizens not only to do efficient and accurate work themselves, but also to demand efficient and accurate work of those whom they place in office. By showing the boy the worthlessness of easily acquired knowledge, we can train the grown man to respect the hard-won judgment of the technically trained expert instead of condemning him on the basis of a half-hour's superficial study. But, greater and more important than all these things put together, a right basis of education will give the man who has facts and arguments on his side a fair chance to frame national public opinion in the face of appeals to class prejudice or class interest.

For the boy who has been trained in school to habits of self-reliant thought will not allow his business or political connections in after life to blind him to the necessity of finding things out for himself. He will not be content to take his ideas at second hand from the newspaper that he likes or from the public speaker who appeals to his prejudices. If he attends a political debate he will listen to speakers on both sides with approximately equal attention. If he trusts the integrity of a judge he will make an honest attempt to use the judge's reasoning to help him in his own efforts to determine what justice requires.

Never were American political passions more bitter than in the spring of 1800. Never were social and sectional animosities more acute than at the time when the Republican party of that day, seeking a campaign issue against President Adams and the Federalists for use in the approaching presidential election, attacked him as a truckler to Great Britain, because he had authorized the extradition of one Thomas Nash who claimed to be an American citizen, but who was "wanted" in England for mutiny and murder. After acrimonious debate in a pretty evenly divided House, John Marshall, afterwards Chief Justice of the United States, defended the conduct of the Administration in a speech of much more than ordinary lucidity, even for Marshall himself. Three remarkable things followed. First, Albert Gallatin, who had led the opposition in the earlier stages of the debate with his usual brilliancy, being called upon by his followers for a reply, said "Answer it yourselves; I think it unanswerable." Second, in a House which the Administration held by only a narrow margin, the Administration was endorsed by a vote of nearly two to one, in a matter which the Opposition all over the country had made a virulent party issue. And finally, Thomas Jefferson, Marshall's bitterest enemy in private as well as in public, who had sought in this issue a powerful means of advancing his own election as President, wrote this brief summary of the debate in his diary: "Livingston, Nicholas and Gallatin distinguished themselves on one side and J. Marshall greatly on the other."

It was this intellectual basis—this objective response of the mind to an appeal for the common good—that allowed the United States of America to remain a single self-governing commonwealth under political conditions which appeared to make such a result impossible. It is this intellectual habit on which England or America or any other free people must rely in dealing with the industrial problems which have come up in the century which has since elapsed. For on the ability of the citizens as a body to entertain the appeal from prejudice to reason, from class interest and class consciousness to national interest and national consciousness, the very existence of democracy depends.

INDEX

Printed in the United States
By Bookmasters